For Corporate Rebels Only

For Corporate Rebels Only

*Why Tomorrow's Leaders are Quiet
Quitting Today*

Dale E Funk

This book is dedicated to Camille and David.

CONTENTS

CHAPTER 1 – PURPOSE OF THIS BOOK

The primary reasons I wrote this book are because I believe:

1. *The ethic of hard work and personal reward for that work are essential components of the human quest for meaning. In its simplest form, hard work may contribute to one's sense of self-worth. In the ideal situation, it may also add to both personal and spiritual growth. In all situations it has the potential to contribute to one's overall quality of life.*

2. *The exploitation and abuse of one's need for meaning by those in power hinders the individual's creativity, spirit, sense of self-worth, and quality of life—and will ultimately lead to the demise of a society.*

This book has been in the back of my mind since the mid-1980s when I first started my career and read a book titled *In Search of Excellence* [1].

My hopes are that those who read it will find the inspiration to reach all of their personal goals. While that may seem simplistic, in today's world we are drawn so many directions that it is often difficult to even discover what might bring us true happiness.

Motivation precedes any action, and while in its simplest form it might be defined as "the will to carry out an action", understanding how to command it in one's own life is a more complex process. The real question may be whether or not one is carrying out one's own will, or that of someone else.

While on the surface it appears that the last forty years have come with an increased understanding of workers' needs, I believe there is still a missing link that needs to be filled if corporations are to keep and maintain their employees for the long haul.

This book is not about organizations and workplace goals though; it is about you, your goals, and finding ultimate satisfaction with your own life. A better understanding of organizations may lead to that end and is thus a large part of this text.

Quiet-quitting, where an employee reduces his work output to the minimum required, and essentially disregards requests for more output than required for the paid worktime has been discussed a lot over the past couple of years. Much of the discussion has been directed negatively towards the millennials with the suggestions that they're, unmotivated, unproductive, lazy, spoiled.

At the very least, I believe once you read this you will have some understanding of why *quiet-quitting* is a reasonable option in certain environments today. And for those who accuse the younger millennials and zillennials of not being motivated, I hope to provide insight as to why *quiet-quitting* may be for the ultimately motivated in today's world.

When I began writing this book, I did not realize what a challenge it would be to convey this information in a meaningful way while keeping the text short. The good news is that there is an extensive body of research supporting the information herein.

I've listened to so many people around my age (64) talk about how the younger generation doesn't have a work ethic and how selfish and demanding they are that I felt this needed some research. The results will likely surprise anyone who buys into that stereotype.

Younger people are humans just like prior generations, and one would expect them to have the same qualities and ambitions as humans who came before them. Would it make sense that they suddenly didn't share the hopes, and dreams of prior generations? Probably not.

Previous generations—including mine, were taught and expected their standard of living to be higher than their parents. Owing to technology, evolution, and society, there's no reason it shouldn't be, but for the first time in the United States, this is not the case.

It struck me that perhaps the millennials had figured something out that was changing in our society and perhaps there was something to be learned from them.

My generation would answer that the millennials simply don't commit themselves, but again, this doesn't make sense. Why wouldn't they commit? Isn't it reasonable to assume that they are as intelligent and motivated as prior generations, and their decisions are based on some logic?

It turns out that my intuition back in the early '80s was at least partially correct, and forty years later the issues that led me to leave the corporate world at a young age have become even more evident as companies have refined their exploitation of the workforce.

In what at first appears to be a paradox, *quiet-quitting* may be for the ultimately motivated, and may make even more sense today than when I used the same technique, though it didn't have a name at the time, forty years ago.

While it's impossible to write a book like this and not share one's own opinion because any interpretation of facts leads to opinions, and sometimes strong emotion, I have attempted to present solid evidence to support the opinions presented.

I also wanted to share facts that might not only serve as a call to action for readers willing to absorb the information, but also empower them to make the changes necessary to remain motivated throughout life.

I have met many talented people who do not reach their full potential in life for the simple reason that they have not directed their talents in a fulfilling manner. In some cases, they just don't believe they can succeed, in others they don't have the tools to recognize their talents, and in others they have not found the motivation or courage to make the changes in their job or career that will lead them to their maximum potential.

As someone with no particular talent, I've relied mostly on motivation to see any level of success in life. Thus, I've spent a great deal of time studying how to remain motivated, so at the very least I hope some insight towards motivation is forthcoming.

I'm excited to share this information with you and hope you find it helpful in attaining your own goals as you take life on.

CHAPTER 2 – SHOULD YOU READ THIS BOOK?

If you're happy with your job and your company, and/or plan to stay there forever this book may not be for you. If on the other hand, you do not feel your current employer, or position will take you to your full potential, you may find some motivation herein.

Before continuing, it's important to understand what this book is, and what it is not.

WHAT THIS BOOK IS NOT

This book is not a statement against hard work, capitalism, materialism, consumerism, religion or for that matter, corporate America. It is not a political statement directed for or against any political party, group, or belief system.

WHAT THIS BOOK IS

This book is a statement against the exploitation of people. It is a statement of how and why you should take control of your life and remove yourself from a corporation or job that is toxic. It is a statement of why many corporations in America will continue to fail both their shareholders and their employees unless they change their priorities with respect to their work force.

A PANDEMIC - A NEW WORLD

Following the event of the Covid pandemic, the world seems to have forever changed, and what we used to think of as normal may no longer exist. Because of that, and the lack of trust in the stability of normalcy, finding the motivation to return to our previous goals and activities is, for some, challenging. The upside of the pandemic is that it inspired many of us to re-evaluate our situations and change our priorities.

The recent changes in society have resulted in numerous new opportunities and now is the perfect time to examine and understand your own motivation in order to take full advantage of this unique time in history.

With the Pandemic came a large increase in *working from home.*

Quiet-quitting, where workers have decided that it no longer makes sense to devote their entire life to a company and have decided to keep their efforts to the minimum required has been around longer but is just now finding its moment.

This phenomenon points to the missing link between the research on how to motivate workers, and how to implement this knowledge, because if it had been properly executed the need for *quiet-quitting* would not exist.

FAULTY RESEARCH OR FAILED IMPLEMENTATION?

This may be a bold statement, but I believe that the last hundred years of research on motivation are failing in most corporations because of reasons that have nothing to do with generational work ethics or an understanding of what motivates people, but rather the current system is unwilling or unable to heed the knowledge and advice that all those years of research have given.

The problem isn't the knowledge base on how to motivate employees, but rather, the improper use of that knowledge.

Part of the problem is that most research on motivation has been carried out by corporations and Government with the sole purpose of controlling people's behavior, with virtually no consideration of maximizing the employee's (human being's) potential.

Given the centralization of wealth in our country, it's unlikely that large corporations are going away anytime soon; hence, *quiet-quitting* is the logical first step in attempting to correct the current misdirection of these corporations.

In my opinion, it has taken us about forty years too long to figure out that *quiet-quitting* is the right answer so my hat is off to the millennials for taking on this problem with these seemingly impenetrable corporations.

My hope is that this book will at the very least empower employees to help these mis-directed corporations learn respect for what their employees bring to the table, and better yet, improve the quality of life of our working class while allowing them to find reward in the utilization of their talents.

Ultimately it boils down to two questions: 1.) Do you feel your talents are being utilized to their fullest? 2.) Do you feel you are being justly compensated by your employers.

If the answer is no to either of these questions you may find this book very interesting.

CHAPTER 3 – THE PSYCHOLOGY OF MOTIVATION

The question around motivation revolves not so much around what one wishes to accomplish as it does why one hopes to accomplish it.

This is something we will return to many times throughout this book because it really is the key to understanding how to make your world the way you want it. Without some background information it won't make as much sense, and you won't be able to apply these principles to your own life.

TYPES OF MOTIVATION

Let's begin by defining the two most basic types of motivation:

1.) *Intrinsic: That which is motivated from within for the sheer pleasure of doing something, or desire to reach a goal. For example, Motivation to learn to play an instrument for the delight of playing without the expectation of ever being paid.* **Result: Taking action based on one's own will to accomplish an action.**

2.) *Extrinsic: That which is motivated from the outside by a positive or negative reward. Examples might be a productivity bonus at work, or avoiding a traffic ticket by following the speed limit.* **Result: Taking action based on someone else's will to accomplish an action.**

It's fair to say that given a preference most of us would choose intrinsic motivation over external. In an ideal world, all of our chosen actions would be based on our desires and enjoyment.

In the real world though, it's likely that most of our actions are motivated by extrinsic factors involving some other entity's will. We work to make money, we put up with bosses who shouldn't be managing people, we often go to a job that we can't stand because we need to make our house payments or meet other financial responsibilities; we follow a lot of rules to avoid penalties, etc. etc.

Historically research on motivation has been carried out with the goal of providing tools to manage and motivate workers for the purpose of increased company profits, and in fact, the general body of research doesn't consider that an individual might learn to use this research for their own personal gain. One of the more important facts that have been established is that beyond a certain level, monetary reward is not a good motivating factor. [2]

Using this knowledge for personal gain is one goal of this book. Understanding this research will allow us to see both why it most often fails in a corporate environment, and how to use it to our own benefit.

The results of the research on motivation indicate that in some cases, monetary reward leads to improved performance, and in other cases it does not.

For tasks that are related to repetitive mechanical work, studies show that providing a monetary-reward or bonus for higher production is quite successful in motivating workers to be more productive. This would include tasks such as assembly line work, or any work where one is "trained" to complete a task.

Because technology has brought robotics into assembly lines, and many repetitive task jobs are disappearing, using money as a means of motivation is less useful than in previous times.

Research studies also show that for jobs involving problem solving and cognitive processing, monetary bonuses do not improve performance or productivity. Given the long history of using bonus pay for improved productivity in industry, it initially came as a surprise to researchers to learn that when higher monetary bonuses were offered, people performed worse on tasks relying on cognitive processing for increased productivity.

It's not that "thinking" people don't want more money, but that the added pressure of trying to solve problems under the gun of a timeline to receive a bonus detracts from the solving of the problems.

Not surprisingly, companies initially took this to mean they didn't need to pay their "professional" employees more for better performance.

At some point however, it was determined that if a worker is paid enough so that he doesn't have to face stress in paying the bills outside of work, he/she will be able to focus on the task at hand, and therefore, should be compensated at a high enough level to reduce financial stress in order to be the most productive.

Without going in depth on the numerous models of how to motivate workers, it's safe to say that most large corporations are still not getting it.

In today's world we find consultants like Simon Sinek, being paid big dollars to tell companies things they already know. He does a nice job too, but this isn't new knowledge. The real problem is that the companies don't listen to him, or at least don't implement his message. As we will see, due to the current structure and philosophy of business, it is unlikely that they will ever listen to his message.

I think back to how disappointed I was in the 1980s upon starting my first job after graduating from Electrical Engineering school.

At that time everyone was reading a book titled "In Search of Excellence,"[1] and it was required reading in the corporation where I was employed. The book was written as a management tool and the authors had studied what they called "excellent" companies and I devoured it hungrily seeking knowledge of how to assist these great companies and find success early in my career.

In short, the authors reasoned that these highly profitable "excellent" companies had the secret to creating a culture that elevated the productivity of the *ordinary* people working there to *extra-ordinary* levels. Thus, if managers could inject these traits into their own organization, they too would have high performers, and ultimately more profit.

That all sounded reasonable, and aside from the fact that it seemed very few of the managers who read the book had a clue what it was saying, there was an emotional stir about it in the media that seemed to empower them.

The contents of that book inspired a complete change in the direction of my life, and I will explain this in the next chapter.

First let's look at several ideas that more recent research has revealed.

HUMAN SATISFACTION

After it was shown that higher monetary rewards did not lead to more productive performance on tasks regarding cognitive reasoning, it was shown that there are other rewards that lead to both better performances, and more personal satisfaction than just money.

1.) *Autonomy — The desire to be self-directed*

2.) *Mastery —The urge to get better at something.*

3.) *Purpose — The intention to achieve a long-term goal.*

See [3]

As the world became increasingly technical and the competition for highly educated employees intensified, use of factors one and three above came into play by way of creating "company cultures."

Autonomy is likely the easiest to relate to because most of us know inherently that we prefer to self-direct rather than to be directed. If we feel we are in control of our own destination, we perform better in general, unless of course our survival is under threat, but in most of today's societies that is rare, and in fact, any improvement in performance due to threatened survival is extremely short-term.

Mastery is an interesting factor because there seems to be something inherent in human nature that seeks this. Strangely, we will spend hours mastering something like the piano even if we know we're never going to get paid, or even if there's no externally measurable benefit to us.

Another example is that humans spend hours playing video games—for what? The sheer delight of mastering the game. The interesting thing is, out of that pleasure came an industry in itself. In fact, it's amazing how much technology has come out of the human's enjoyment for mastery alone, often with no economic benefit to those who created it.

Clearly this is an area that a large corporation would gain benefit from exploiting, and as an engineer, I can vouch that it keeps many technical people in their jobs even when the working conditions aren't so great. With most jobs in today's world centering around technical expertise, this trait alone contributes positively to keeping workers because as one masters a coding language or database, it is difficult to want to leave to another job.

Purpose has recently become a huge area of competition to attract employees, and funding in general. We find it in all walks of life from a child on You Tube presenting the safest toys for children to crowd funding sites like GoFundMe, to Greta Thunberg urging us to save the planet, to advertisements showing abused animals, all appealing to the human need for a sense of purpose.

In their quest for employees and customers, companies now advertise that they give a percentage of income to one charity or another, are working towards zero carbon output, or are the pinnacle of inclusiveness, or any number of methods to tap into their potential customers' or employees' sense of purpose in life.

With social media, the human need for purpose is being exploited for monetary gains like no other time in history, with much of this due to the research on how to motivate people to action.

The research indicates that the three factors above are what are needed to motivate people to accomplish high productivity in the workplace as well. In fact, it's been shown that with these factors present, a person is unlikely to quit a job, even when offered another job at substantially higher pay.

With all this research on motivation, and all this action to make sure our needs are being met, you might ask: Why are the millennials so unmotivated, and how can *quiet-quitting* somehow be equated with being motivated?

Simon Sinek, hits the nail on the head in a keynote John C. Maxell's Live2Lead event in Atlanta, Georgia, October 7, 2016 entitled "Most Leaders Don't Even Know the Game They're In' [4]

Here, he speaks about what he calls the *infinite game*. Sinek explains that in a finite game there is a clear-cut winner and loser, but in an infinite game such as business, which ultimately outlasts all players, the winner is really the one who stays in the game the longest. In essence, because most businesses are playing to win on a very short-term basis, their methods are not likely sustainable and they will ultimately drop out of the game, whereas the business whose goal is simply to remain in the game wins by default because it remains in business.

This to me, is one of the most philosophical presentations on why companies are failing their employees and destined to fail themselves in the long run, as he points out specific methods that companies might initiate to improve their most valuable asset—their employees. Perhaps the more profound truth in this presentation is simply the title: "Most Leaders Don't Even Know the Game They're In."

He's spot on. Much like back in the eighties, most of the corporate managers and leaders who are required to read these leadership books and attend leadership seminars are clueless. They're doing it because they have to. They're doing it because someone told them it will help their department make more money, or they feel it will improve their resume for their next promotion. They're doing it because their company hired a consultant, and the seminar or lecture was mandatory.

Sinek professes a very direct message, and though they pay him as a consultant, they won't listen. The reason they won't listen is because he's suggesting that money should not be the primary focus of a company, and the only reason they hire him is the hopes of increased profits. In a way, he poses what in most of their minds is **a paradox that cannot be resolved**.

The one thing that hasn't changed in my life is the fact that for a business, **more money is the primary driver**, and the problem with that is that there is never enough money in the minds of those trying to generate a profit. As Sinek points out, this motive can only lead to failure in the long run. Why? Because there can only be more money for a limited amount of time.

The system as it stands cannot revise itself regardless of what the consultants or HR department say because the companies are controlled by MBAs, Accountants, and Attorneys with one goal, and that is to generate higher profits than the previous quarter. The MBAs and accountants in charge of generating profits do not concern themselves with the knowledge of employee retention consultants, nor do they entertain the notion of a long-term plan, so talking about an infinite game is outside of their mind-space.

Yet... just like the inspirational speakers and writers of the eighties, large corporations pay consultants to speak to their managers, to bring a message that will improve their company's profitability, and similar to the eighties, the managers nod their head, and for a moment, they feel empowered. But only for a moment because, in fact, our system cannot step back from next quarter's profits and is not wired to process or implement any message that might require stepping away from that notion.

<u>Just because the message is a fleeting thought in the minds of the corporate managers, and likely the corporation itself, does not mean that you can't take this message to heart and incorporate it in your own life, and use it to your own benefit</u>. You can take control of your own life. I expect the only way to benefit from this knowledge is by making your life "yours" and changing the way you view your employer, especially if your employer is a large corporation.

The next chapter delves into some history of how much of your life a corporation would like to own, and how they might go about obtaining that portion.

Have you considered how much of your energy you are willing to give to your employer, or how you decided when or why to set limits as to what you will give?

CHAPTER 4 – A FIRST CALL TO ACTION

I'm going to step back in time to the 80s for a moment and share with you what I considered a call to action at the time, and something that forever changed my future. Now with forty more years of research, it will be interesting to hear your thoughts on it after you have read this—if you decide to share them with me, and I hope you will.

THE BEGINNING

When written, the book *In Search of Excellence,* was considered groundbreaking. It provided insights into how to obtain maximum productivity from employees.

Much of the research was oriented around the idea that the more time the employee was thinking about solving work problems, or the more of the employee's energy that was expended towards the company, the more the company stood to gain profits.

Stated simply, there are 24 hours in a day comprising 100% of one's energy and the goal of the company is to have their employees expend as much of that energy as possible meeting company needs. The optimum would be 100% of the employee's energy. Though of course that's not possible, there are many material and psychological techniques to maximize this capture of energy.

Recommendations include creating an environment that would keep the attention of the employees directed towards the company. For example, many companies changed their corporate offices into a "campus" style environment with gyms, lounges, nature walks, etc. On campus weekend social activities were another method of keeping the company's needs at the forefront of the employee's mindset. This in and of itself is not sinister and at times both employee and employer stand to benefit.

However, in researching these "excellent" companies, the authors learned that the successful ones took advantage of two very paradoxical human needs. The need for self-determination (autonomy—where a person controls their own work), and the need for security.

As presented in *In Search of Excellence*: "At the same time we are almost too willing to yield to institutions that give us meaning and thus a sense of security, we also want self-determination…." "….This is certainly irrational. Yet, those who don't learn to somehow manage the tension are, in fact, technically insane."[1]

Those are the words of the authors of *In Search of Excellence*. Let that soak in because it's somewhat key to the whole discussion.

The next paragraphs state: "Psychologists study the need for self-determination in a field called 'illusion of control.'" Stated simply, findings of the studies indicate that if people think they have even modest personal control over their destinies, they will persist at tasks. "They will do better at them. They will become committed to them." [1]

What does this mean? It seems the consequences of the preceding paragraphs went largely unnoticed, yet the implications are enormous. Interestingly, it never came up in our management discussion groups at the time.

The next paragraph is my interpretation of what the authors said, but feel free to disagree.

To attain maximum productivity, employees have to not only buy into the illusion of having security, but also that of having control over their own destiny, two paradoxical situations, or—to reach maximum productivity in one of these institutions, the employee must reach a state as defined in the psychological world as "technically insane."

Hmm. Let's stop and scratch our heads on that one again. Though nobody seemed to pay much attention to it at the time, for me it rang an alarm bell. **I suppose it's worth asking if one wishes to live in a world where those in control have a primary goal to keep us in a state defined as "technically insane" in our one trip through life.**

If you've seen the satirical Jim Carrey movie, "The Truman Show," you realize that living in an illusion can be quite comfortable, until or unless the illusion is shattered. If the illusion were maintained from cradle to grave, great, but in today's rapidly changing world that's unlikely.

At this point we're left with two choices regarding our beliefs:

1.) *We can deny the paradox stated by the psychological research and reach a resolution by believing that we really do have both control, and security, in which case according to the psychological theories, we're insane.*

2.) *We can accept the truth of the paradox, which entails no longer believing that the institutions we consider our "excellent" companies are providing us with what they claim. In other words—they're lying to us to make us more productive.*

The illusions of security and autonomy seem to have been shattered repeatedly by these companies, and yet they still persist in describing themselves as near Utopian organizations in their job descriptions and recruitment methods.

Is it any wonder that an entire generation has become so cynical? Is it any wonder that we saw movements like *Occupy Wall Street*, or more recently, the *quiet-quitting* movement?

So — Who's right? The millennials, for not believing they should bust their asses for these corporations, or those in previous generations who kept believing in them throughout the eighties, nineties, and beyond, and now believe the millennials are just lazy.

In defense of our older generations, most of us were raised by the Post WWII generation that believed in both companies and politicians back in the days when both gave us some reasons to believe they might have our best interest in mind, or at least believe we deserved a life beyond our working years.

There was a time when corporations provided both job security and retirement for those who stayed with them. In today's world, both of those perks are seen as profit reducers.

One problem with completely accepting the truth is that it's very uncomfortable. Plus, nobody really wants to be a cynic at heart. **But we cannot deny the fact that it is**

a well thought out volitional lie, devised by psychologists who taught the lie to corporate management for the sole purpose of manipulating behavior into productivity through deception for the purpose of creating profits for the company with full disregard of the best interests of the employees, and in many cases damaging employees' lives —*And the lie continues today.*

Another problem is that these corporations carry a lot of wealth, power and resources as well as jobs. While most have clearly broken their promise and will continue to do so when it suits their own best interest, so do most politicians. Does that stop us from voting? So far it doesn't, but the key is to not deny the truth of and results of their actions, and finally to never foolishly give credence to their rhetoric.

CHAPTER 5 – A SECOND CALL TO ACTION

WHY IT'S SO OBVIOUS

Gen "X" saw it coming, but the millennials got it figured out and how could they not? They have seen one lie after another, and somehow throughout it all, the leaders of the corporations keep getting higher salaries, the richest people in the world keep getting richer at a pace that outpaces inflation, the marketing department continues to bombard the public with advertisements carrying buzz phrases that paint non-existent utopian pictures while the workers' wages keep lagging behind inflation in a slow devolution towards a lower standard of living for the working class. And we're surprised when someone stands up to this intentional illusion. In reality, there would likely be less resistance with a simple, truthful authoritarian rule than one that continuously lies.

While Jeff Bezos' $500 million dollar yacht is so big that a bridge would have to be dismantled to get the finished boat out of port in the Netherlands, workers in Amazon warehouses are begging for safe and healthy work conditions.

With all due respect to the successful businessmen who acquire mansions, yachts, and eons of wealth, I would offer that the success should not be at the expense of the risk and health of their employees and/or the general population. That approach has been carried out in the past by many societies and the end results were never favorable to mankind. In the case of Amazon, they would still be making plenty of money, even if they treated their employees with respect.

Starbucks, who is known for their progressive stances, is facing unionization of workers. What? Isn't this the company where everyone wanted to work? The company of inclusiveness?

A brief look at history suggests that unions form when workers are getting screwed. Happy workers don't form unions.

The question is why has Starbucks fought so hard against unions if the workers are being taken care of as well as the company claims. Are the workers really getting too wealthy working at Starbucks?

Again, strength only comes in numbers. Starbucks is a service company that still relies on humans, and though they could certainly devise a robotic latte delivery system, it wouldn't be the Starbucks we know and love.

They forgot that it's not up to the company CEO and his 2021 39% increase in salary to 20.4 million dollars/year, to decide if the meager cost-of- living increase given to the baristas was sufficient to survive on. It's really up to the employees, and that's why they're going on strike. If most or all of the workers think they're getting screwed, they probably are, and history repeats itself with the formation of unions.

The real problems occur when the leadership, who is already making multi-millions of dollars/year, is of the ilk that believe they deserve 40% raises while employees deserve at best a raise slightly less than the rate of inflation.[5]

Let's go back to the $500 million dollar yacht. While this blatant display stirs emotions, it's really a small drop in the bucket when the true wealth of Jeff Bezos is considered. The problems arise when these moguls believe their genius entitles them to that wealth but lose touch with the working class that is enabling their success.

As consumers we don't see that side of the business and find it very difficult to turn away from the lower costs of purchasing these goods as long as it's not at our own expense.

Any reader who doesn't want to choose the lowest cost selection for any item raise your hand now. (Where do you stand?) I guess you could say that makes us all capitalists at heart, and if nothing else we understand why these corporations attempt to hoard the wealth, for we as consumers rarely consider the working conditions in the country or factory that an item was produced to bring us low prices, we only consider the price we are paying.

We too look out for our best interest by selecting the lowest cost for any product, which in many cases means we encourage the exploitation of these workers. It appears that capitalism is a basic foundation of human nature.

Let's look at working conditions and Amazon's answer. [6]

 "I couldn't handle it. I'm a human being, not a robot." [6]

"You're being tracked by a computer the entire time you're there. You don't get reported or written up by managers. You get written up by an algorithm." [6]

"…if there is too much time elapsed between items, the computer will know this, will write you up, and you will get fired." [6]

An amazon spokesperson indicated that coaching is provided to under-performing workers.

One worker said "….it reminded him of prison – not least because of the 20-minute wait to get through security in and out of the facility." [6]

He further stated: "I would rather go back to a state correctional facility and work for 18 cents an hour than do that job." [6]

The problem in this situation is defining 'under-performing' workers. When is a worker underperforming? Pushing workers to the brink is nothing new in the world of industry, it was commonplace at the beginning of the industrial revolution, and slave labor is still common in other countries, many of which we all happily purchase low-cost goods from.

We don't seem to mind abuse of labor except when it's at our own expense. The problem is, with globalization it may lead to our own demise. Workers in the United States are now being required to compete with the low-cost labor in other countries.

With the event of AI computer monitoring of human labor and the development of efficiency algorithms, we can't help but wonder if it's the efficiency created by the genius of a businessman, or simply a new way to exploit human capital in a way that allows those in power to further insulate themselves from humanity.

This last quote amply demonstrates the spiraling effects of a fear-based work environment as in Amazon:

"Other Amazon workers at the New York City warehouse were reluctant to speak on the record for fear of retaliation, but also reported unaddressed safety concerns and frequent worker injuries." [6]

Once fear governs a worker's willingness to come forward, all bets are off. This places us on the same level as countries that exploit labor beyond reason because workers feel they have nowhere to turn. Is this where we're headed as a society? Once we reach that point, *quiet-quitting* will no longer be an option. The time is now, before it's too late.

Here is another example from recent news involving an email from new Twitter owner, Elon Musk, sent to his employees. By the time this book is printed, this will be old news and the results will be in, but let's speculate.

"Going forward, to build a breakthrough Twitter 2.0 and succeed in an increasingly competitive world, we will need to be extremely hardcore," the email read. "This will mean working long hours at high intensity. Only exceptional performance will constitute a passing grade."[7]

The question that comes to mind is who is competing with who? In this case it appears Mr. Musk is trying to set up a situation where his employees can compete with each other to see who will work the longest hours for him and decide whether or not they get to stay on his payroll and help him maintain his position as the richest man in the world. Certainly, it's not difficult to understand the *self-appointed savior* of the world ego created by such wealth, but the question is whether or not it is a worker's obligation to feed it, or whether Twitter would be better served if the entire staff either quit, or *quiet-quit.*

It's one thing to compete in professional athletics and make millions of dollars per year, but it's quite another to be placed in the ring against other employees, in a situation akin to the Squid Games, with the simple hopes of holding onto a job.

The message appears to be: **Give everything you have to your work, or end up with nothing.** The problem with this "all or nothing" approach is that it leads to fear of losing what we do have. While it may facilitate higher paid employees to compete, the fear of losing what they already have has been proven to ultimately lead to inferior performance.

Perhaps the elitist view is that the working class should be forced to compete to serve as entertainment for the uber-wealthy while making them wealthier. Perhaps the idea is to allow the working class the illusion of having material success in the form of high mortgages and payments to keep them competing in the ring, while never having the benefit of security. The problem is, when the layoffs come, the mortgages can't be paid and the illusion disappears. Perhaps it is the first step towards the Squid Game [8]. Remember, similar games were played in the past by the Romans.

This general trend has been going on since the eighties when large holding companies began buying smaller companies with complete disregard for the employees or their histories at the company for the sheer profit factor and is only now maturing.

I can attest, from my own experience, that seeing co-workers laid off in waves around you while you are facing a mortgage and raising children is quite daunting.

During the 80's, corporations also moved away from company paid retirement plans and began to force employees to contribute to their own, while not increasing wages, all the while encouraging them to invest their retirement money into company stock dangling a small company match as a lure.

This was all sanctioned and encouraged by the Federal government with their 401K incentives that limited retirement investments into stock portfolios and ETF type investments and further bolstered corporate America with our retirement funds.

ENRON was one of the more egregious examples of how easily employees' investments could be stolen, as well as how easily such policies could be implemented. In that case, employees who had worked in companies for their entire careers lost everything they had saved for retirement.

Unfortunately, our society has come to rely on these large corporations for both our economy and our jobs, and while their talking points may include "Social Responsibility", the evidence suggests that this responsibility is only present when it's needed as a talking point to attract employees or investors to further their profits.

CHAPTER 6 – A FINAL CALL TO ACTION

A WELL-DEFINED PLAYING FIELD

The economic platform that Milton Friedman put forth in the 70's was a simple one. It stated that the function of a business is to make profit—period. That's it—nothing more. Leave the ethics, the social responsibility, and so forth to the government. The MBAs and Accountants are still taught this so their actions should come as no real surprise.

For starters, we need to face the fact that this approach of teaching business certainly attracts, and likely fuels a sociopathic type of personality given that morals and ethics (by definition) are not to be included in the decision process when seeking monetary gains from any business venture.

We also need to accept that this necessarily creates the need for government regulation in order to maintain some semblance of order, because it is only the laws that will set a limit on the behavior of a business. That's a tall order for the government, but we've asked for it.

Probably the only upside to this type of setup is that it's a *well-defined playing field with clearly stated rules*. The downside is that it results in massive government regulations with the corporations somehow always staying one step ahead of the rules in a game of cat and mouse that leads to an endless formation of bureaucracy in the government.

CREATING THE LIE

The conflict between employees perceived and actual roles began during the tech years when there was extreme competition for highly educated technical workers and has continued as technology has demanded workers with higher levels of training and education.

This was when the human resource folks realized they needed to sell their company to prospective employees in order to fill positions. As the movement expanded, social responsibility, company mission, and other talking points entered the vocabulary as a means of creating an illusion that might attract potential employees and investors.

The problem is that the illusions created by the marketing departments to attract employees, advertisers, and investors, for the most part, have little to do with the actual businesses and how they're run.

This is easier for investors to accept than employees because ultimately investors are there for the same reason as the business itself: to make money. While it might be preferable to have a company aligned with one's own mission and belief system, if it is showing limited returns, investors will not continue investing.

While companies complain about regulations and labor laws, Milton Friedman's economic model and definition of the purpose of a business made it fairly clear that without them, we'd already be back to peasant labor because businesses are not to concern themselves with morals or ethics.

Instead, through an elaborate collusion between government and banks involving student loans, mortgages, and credit cards, the working class is now serving the system in more of an indentured servant role to feed the isolated towers of wealth that control most of congress.

While many individual entrepreneurs carry strong moral and ethical values and do in fact care for their employees, these values are rare in large publicly traded companies where the only thing that matters is quarterly earnings and annual profits. In these cases, the highly paid CEOs are not trained to worry about morals or ethics, but rather to make money period, and to try to stay out of jail in the meantime.

A DEVELOPING OLIGARCHY?

What happens when Congress is the only entity to regulate corporations, but becomes governed by lobbyists of these large entities? Given that both parties seem equally guilty of accepting this money, it's safe to say that the more Congress is controlled by lobbyists, the more they are controlled by big money, and thus, the more their interests tend to align with the companies who by definition of being a business have no morals or ethics. Needless to say, this problem is both evident and prevalent in the United States.

The corporatization of healthcare over the past twenty years is giving us a real time demonstration of this process and how by industrializing a service of heart by handing control to MBAs, Attorneys and Accountants, humanity can be both forgotten and destroyed in the name of profits.

While previously governed by Physicians who were also highly trained in morals and ethics, the change in control to non-healthcare educated administrators who's only job is to develop a profit center has led to a devastating healthcare system that is providing progressively lower quality of care and having more and more difficulty retaining employees.

One of the major reasons is because the rules are no longer defined by healthcare providers, the providers themselves spend most of their time sorting through these rules in their quest for payment and are no longer allowed to simply perform their job of taking care of patients.

Every attempt to reel this system back in is failing in the United States, seemingly because it's hopelessly controlled by those seeking to profit from it with no concern for the long-term viability of the model, or those who are damaged along the way.

The result is a steady decline in life expectancy, an increase in infant death rates, increased drug addiction, and a health insurance system licensed to extort the highest population (the working middle class). With this system it's no surprise a recent study shows that medical errors are now the third leading cause of death in the United States.[9]

Excuse me? Yes…. This is very difficult to believe for those of us who believe in this country as being the best in the world. "The medical coding system was designed to maximize billing for physician services, not to collect national health statistics, as it is currently being used."

[9], says Makary in this article, explaining why it's just now being discovered that the 3rd leading cause of death is due to medical errors.

Don't want to believe it? OK, that's your choice, but denial does not make a better system.

Could Big Pharma's lobbying effort be the reason that our country pays so much for medicine when compared to any other country in the world, or why our Country which is 5% of the world population uses 90% of the opioid drugs produced in the world. Could the Healthcare insurance lobbyists have anything to do with the fact that when you tell anyone from another country what your healthcare premiums and deductibles are they have difficulty believing it, especially given the low ranking of 37th in the world of the U.S. medical system?

Has it become a one-way street where the working middle class citizens are to pay for everything via premiums and taxes while the corporations and large stockholders continue to separate themselves with wealth while lobbying to unburden themselves of any financial responsibility via middle class tax programs?

Why does this surprise people? This is what happens when corporations control a government via lobbying funds to Congress. Any legislation passed must guarantee the Congressmen, the corporations, and the elite will all get wealthier. It seems to be to the demise of small independent businesses, and the middle class. This is a non-partisan issue. Both sides are equally guilty.

The question is: What will be the end product of all of this?

We have placed businesses in a paradox in that if they don't show quarterly profit increases their stock prices will go down and, in such a rapidly changing economy, companies can go out of business overnight. Perhaps this model might also be defined as some sort of "insanity".

Yet we all seem surprised with the outcome we're seeing, and especially the backlash from the millennials regarding donating their minds and lives to corporate greed. We all seem surprised that they're not enjoying the fact that they no longer see the opportunity that previous generations saw in this country due to the tentacles of the corporation extending into and attempting to extinguish every chance they might have.

Though it's certainly more comfortable to buy into the corporate illusion, because as psychologists pointed out, we will gladly live in a paradox if we are convinced that our lives have meaning, at some point we can't deny the evidence. And the evidence is that not only do we not have autonomy, but we don't have security, and to what extent the rhetoric about social responsibility has any merit is questionable in most cases.

In fact, the evidence suggests that, from the standpoint of a corporation, our only purpose as living beings whether as an employee, or paying customer, is to increase their profits.

Is this the reason we are alive? Is this what we want our legacy to be—to increase the profits of corporations?

This certainly causes one to question the direction of humanity, and while *quiet-quitting* might offer us an exit from the apparent insanity, alone it doesn't offer us much hope for an improved life, which is also a natural human need and desire.

It may be that looking into the lives of those who've found other options might help us blaze a path, but at the very least, we need to understand that in the end, we the general population, have the power, though perhaps not via a vote or revolution, but by simply refusing to be a part of the insanity.

Unfortunately, the power only comes in numbers. For example, if every employee at Amazon decides they will intentionally move less pieces than the robot monitor requires then the standard of productivity could be reset.

That is unlikely to happen, but right now we are faced with the option of competing with each other on an artificial playing field created to make the wealthy wealthier or quitting and leaving them on their own to run their companies, or…. simply *quiet-quitting*, and not giving them more of our lives than they fairly deserve.

So why do workers allow the greed and apparent need for power of these large institutions, or in some cases business moguls to control them. More often than not, it is fear, and as a society we need to evaluate whether or not a fear-based life is healthy for our citizens. As individuals, we each need to determine whether or not it is serving our personal needs.

Unfortunately, with the billions of corporate dollars lobbying our congressman, we can no longer rely on government to protect our workforce from these predatory practices.

The abuse of human capital is the oldest misuse of capitalism, but we don't need to return to those days. Today is the time of responsible capitalism. It is up to us to fight this battle before it's too late.

It's just as important that our leaders recognize the need for change because continuing on this course will surely lead to the demise of a great society.

Unfortunately, at this point our leaders are not recognizing it, and unless we the people make a clear stand the trend will continue.

CHAPTER 7 – TO THE TUNE OF WHO'S DRUMMER?

We're all familiar with the saying "He marches to the tune of a different drummer" or "He marches to the tune of his own drummer."

Most of us believe we are marching to the tune of our own drummer, but we've all known someone who simply does his/her own thing regardless of what the rest of the world is doing.

If you've seen the movie, "The Social Dilemma," you may question how much your world is being manipulated. The movie made it clear that with the use of cell-phones, social media sites, and simple internet searches, the artificial based intelligence that monitors our every action and tracks our whereabouts gets to know us very well, and uses the information to determine what we will be exposed to online. This includes everything from which news stories we will see, to the advertisements for movies, products, services, and entertainment that are shown to us in our searches and news feeds.

The truth about any of us is that we only have the ability to judge the world through the information we have processed and we can only process the information that we are exposed to. If the information we're privy to is governed in a way to reinforce our notions, we are unlikely to ever be exposed to a broader view, let alone change our notions or worldview.

From that standpoint we do march to the tune of our own drummer, but the problem is, as information is funneled to us, our drummer receives limited exposure to new ideas and thoughts, so may not be able to create a new beat, even when one is needed. The danger is when controlled in such a manner that many of us are marching in cadence, we may be serving as soldiers in an army we don't even know exists.

Yes, we have our own thoughts, but much like Jim Carrey in the Truman show, if we don't see the outside world, we're unlikely to even understand its existence, let alone make sense of it. Furthermore, if our narrow illusion is shattered, we're likely to be at a loss as to how to function.

Something else that was discovered in the book "In Search of Excellence" was that even though an employee might be highly productive in one *excellent* company, the employee was much less likely to perform well in a different environment after being completely socialized into the reward system and illusion created by the initial company.

While the solution seems obvious, it goes completely against human nature to accept that our own thoughts might be the product of outside forces, might be limited to the environment we live in, and might not apply if we had access to a broader knowledge base. It is even more difficult to take the necessary actions to seek a wider set of data.

This is true for all humans, and because of this, rather than entertain new ideas or compromise with those who have opposing ideas, we tend to hunker down on narrow belief systems that may apply in our given circumstances but may not be held elsewhere.

Most of us believe we have open minds, and we tend to believe it is those who disagree with our belief system or haven't been properly exposed to it that are narrow minded. We just personally happen to know that they are wrong, and if they'd only open their minds the world would be a better place because they'd see it our way.

Now picture Artificial Intelligence systems molding themselves to attract employees into a company by feeding the potential employees a value system tailored to popular needs of potential employees. Once in the company, the employee is only exposed to the information that fits his/her needs. This may sound a bit far-fetched, but in fact, it's already happening.

One current example (from personal experience) is in the Medical fields where good-hearted healthcare providers provide assessments, and subsequently those assessments are altered to increase billing. The healthcare provider is hired with the belief that her/his professional expertise is the reason, but often the workers are only hired because the particular license is necessary to have on record in order to create billings. While the worker is trying to provide quality care that is fair to both the patient and the payer, the mission of the administrators is to maximize billing and extract as much money as possible from the healthcare system. This is often done without the knowledge of the healthcare provider. In some cases, the provider is placed in a position where she/he can either agree to the alterations on the assessments, or be let go (though the applied pressure is a bit more subtle than that).

The HIPPA rules prevent healthcare workers from keeping a record (evidence) if they learn of the fraud, and in fact reporting will likely destroy their career. Interestingly, we all wonder why our healthcare system is so expensive while those in charge have created an open cookie jar and expect honesty from the thieves.

Of course, we tend not to believe that this will ever happen to us, but the snag is that if it does, we are unlikely to realize it until it's too late, and it's not often easy to remove oneself from such situations when life's financial obligations exist. In many cases the corporations go to great lengths to make sure it's the individual worker who is implicated when fraud is detected, and not the organization.

CHAPTER 8 – WHAT'S YOUR MINISTRY?

Let's look at a few people that truly did march to the tune of their own drummer. Some such people become rich and famous, but this is rare. It's rare, because though some gain fame or fortune, most people who march to the tune of their own drummer aren't seeking either.

AUNTIE BIRDIE

The title for this chapter came from a lady who went by the name Auntie Birdie. She raised and sold birds. When I first met her, she asked me: "What's your ministry?"

It threw me off because I only associated a ministry with some sort of religion, but I eventually realized she was asking: "How do you serve?" I told her I was a Physical Therapist, and she seemed to approve. We visited her because we wanted to get a cockatiel for our children.

We were welcomed into her home, which seemed to have birds and feathers in every room. Some in open cages, some outside of cages, and some in closed cages.

Some were rescue birds that had come from stressful situations.

We explained that we'd like a grey cockatiel because we'd heard they were more likely to talk. She didn't answer but took us to her kitchen and sat us at her table. Shortly after, she brought in a group of young cockatiels and set them on the table. She explained that we couldn't choose a bird, it had to choose us. Meanwhile, she positioned us such that the birds would all run around our hands, etc. Slowly, one in particular seemed to climb on my daughter's hands and remain, while the others seemed to stay a bit more distant. Auntie Birdie nodded approvingly, and soon we were on our way with a young albino cockatiel.

This was in the winter around Christmas. We were so excited we took the bird to our Christmas dinner. Several days later it appeared that the bird was not doing well. We phoned Auntie Birdie and she had us bring the bird to her home. She phoned her husband who was a Physician. He rushed home from work to meet us and quickly gave the bird an injection. That evening it seemed to be doing better, but within a few days it passed away.

Auntie Birdie felt as bad as we did and allowed us to repeat the process so we ended up with another bird at no charge.

Why this story? The story stuck with me because at the time I was starting a family and my primary concern was being able to pay for everything, save for retirement, etc. etc. It struck me as peculiar that she seemed so eccentric, and to some extent her husband as well, as even though a working physician, both of their hearts seemed dedicated to their ministry which was to care for the birds and the people that enjoyed them. In fact, most of Auntie Birdie's time was donated to taking birds to nursing homes, and assisted living centers for senior citizens to enjoy. Taking care of birds and bringing a moment of joy to another human was her ministry and it served her and others well in her community. She didn't care about money. A far cry from any corporate goal.

BOB ROSS

Nearly everyone knows about Bob Ross and his happy little trees. His show was widespread on Public Television.

What a lot of people don't know is that Bob Ross had been in the Army, and after having served as a Sergeant where he had to order people around, he decided that upon leaving the military he would never raise his voice again.

If you've seen his show, his paintings, and the amount of people who learned his technique, you know the influence he had over the years.

While he made a good living, his ministry was to bring people happiness by showing them they too could be creative. The money was secondary to him. Possibly because of that, others around him ended up with most of the money from his work.

People are still watching him paint his trees, and learning his techniques via his shows, he's become somewhat of an internet sensation, and those interested in the money are still capitalizing from his talent.

Why this story? Without ever focusing on money, the ministry of Bob Ross is still moving audiences nearly thirty years after his death. While most of us don't have such talents or audience, we will all leave a legacy of some sort or another. We each need to ask ourselves every day if our current actions and position are helping create the legacy we want.

OPRAH WINFREY

Everyone knows Oprah so many may wonder why I'm including her here. She's the perfect example of what marching to the tune of one's own drummer can lead to even in the face of extreme odds. There must be a lesson here.

Her mother was a poor teenager who lived in a rural part of Tennessee. She spent time living with her grandmother, and also her father. Due to poverty, she wore dresses made of potato sacks to school. She states she was abused by a cousin, uncle, and family friend starting at nine years old. To escape this, she ran away at thirteen years old. She became pregnant at fourteen and gave birth prematurely to a son who died. This paragraph hardly does justice to what this child we now know as Oprah, the billionaire, really went through.

Let's ask ourselves where Oprah would be in life if she didn't march to the tune of her own drummer. Would Oprah be the richest African-American of the 20th century if she followed the norm? Would Oprah have ever been dubbed the most influential woman in the world if she had accepted any level of what life had dealt her?

Imagine for a moment a young black woman starting out in media and going up against the likes of Phil Donahue, in a world dominated by white males. If anyone ever thinks that any part of Oprah's world was handed to her, or that there weren't multiples forces trying to keep the world she has created for herself from her, think again.

Consider for a moment where Oprah would be today if she had focused on the barriers between her and her goals and all that made her a victim rather than her drive and talent. She was poor, she was black, she was a female, and many in the business found reasons to keep her down.

Why this story? When you feel like a victim, and the world is against you, and you're not sure how you'll find the strength to carry on independently, compare the obstacles you face in life to those of this amazing lady and you're sure to find the inspiration to get up and pound on that drum for another day. When you see the wrongs around you keep going the direction that you know is right.[10]

MY BROTHER MIKE

At forty-nine years old, with two children and a wife at home, my brother was diagnosed with a glioblastoma, a terminal brain tumor for which there is no cure. He was given 9-14 months to live. Overnight his life changed from planning his next home project, worrying about paying for kids' college, and thinking how one day he'd be retired with grandchildren to knowing he would be dead soon and never get to enjoy retirement or grandchildren.

Though he lived a few years longer than his initial diagnosis suggested, his future was defined every sixty days by an MRI, with the knowledge that one day the results would tell him he had about three months left. Sure enough, that day did come, and he died shortly thereafter.

The crazy thing is, even though he was disappointed about his life being shortened, he told me that the brain tumor was the best thing that ever happened to him.

He said it had caused him to completely re-evaluate his life, values, and his priorities. Suddenly, making money, having a bigger house, a fancier car, etc. etc. all had no value in his life because he knew something that most of us live in denial about. He knew life is short and not only do more material goods and wealth not matter when one is dead, beyond meeting basic needs they don't make life happier when one is alive. We're all going to be dead soon, most of us just haven't had to face that.

Having and showing material wealth doesn't lead to a happier or higher quality of life, especially when it's coupled with the stress of monthly payments and subjecting a good portion of our life to someone else's control. Corporations place us in a position that to present the illusion of wealth we have to allow their control.

Why this story? Why is it, that we need to be facing 100% imminent death in the near future in order to understand what's really important? If knowing we're going to be dead soon makes us realize that none of what we thought was important really matters, why be miserable working to assist in an illusion while we're living? Or better yet; why allow an institution to govern our happiness by manipulating our fears so that they might profit? Even better; why allow social norms or political parties to govern our happiness? Why not just bang out a tune on your own drum?

If you knew you were dying within a year, would you live your life the same as you do now?

Don't confuse what I'm saying. Working hard is a virtue. The questions is: Who should gain from that virtue?

How can it be that knowing you are dying soon can be the best thing that ever happened to you? How can it cause one to completely change one's ministry? Would your life be happier if you knew you were dying soon?

If that's what it takes, something is missing in our societal values or cultural values. Are we so deep in denial of our limited time and so lost in our value of wealth and material goods that unless faced with imminent death we are unable to set our priorities straight?

As a final note I want to refer to this article about Bhutan, a country we will talk about more in later chapters. Interestingly, in Bhutan they recommend thinking about death daily, as facing this reality without facing imminent death might help keep the brevity of life as an influence on how we live it.[11]

What's your ministry? What tune are you marching to? What is the purpose of your life? Why are you living? Why do you want to continue to live?

CHAPTER 9 - YOUR Drummer

One of the keys to finding a way out of the madness is to know your own drumbeat. Supposing you do, the next and perhaps the most difficult step is to not care what others think of you.

In our society, this is easy to do when one is reaping the rewards of financial and material success as one is envied by others, but much more difficult at a time when one is vulnerable. Whether or not we show it, most of us are vulnerable most of the time.

One peculiar factor about human nature, at least in our society, is how much people enjoy being critical of others. The truth is, most of those who are highly critical are unable to produce anything original, are often envious, and find release in putting others down. Large companies capitalize on this characteristic of humans by making them feel elite and special while working in their corporate environment.

While it's well known that most of the hatred encountered online comes from the dissatisfaction people have with their own lives, it still hurts to be a victim of these attacks. Unfortunately, with social media the assaults can be hateful and hurtful, and much of this is rooted in the artificial form of happiness and self-satisfaction people present while internally they feel worthless and are full of self-hatred.

It's also likely that your work and social circle will not understand if you change your approach, especially if it's a drastic change. Because of this, it requires even more courage.

One technique used by corporations is to instill a feeling of pride, or superiority in their workers. Once within the confines of such a "work bubble", or in some cases "career bubble", the employees often live in that illusion of superiority and can be quite vicious towards anyone considering leaving, and quickly write off anyone who does leave. I found this to be particularly true in my field of engineering, but I'm sure others are similar.

Part of this pride is instilled to make anyone considering leaving feel as if they are failing because they "couldn't hack it" if they want to leave. It's rare that these employees realize that this behavior is due to their being manipulated by the institution in order to maintain their loyalty and focus rather than any personal shortcomings of the person leaving.

In today's world of social pressure, peer pressure, political correctness, and multitudes of outside forces vying to direct us, it requires a lot of courage to do anything that's not conforming to some societal standard or social norm of those around us. Likewise, it's difficult to accept that others will criticize and view one as inferior if one doesn't buy into the group standards, regardless of the group. This is simply due to humans' need for self-value in their own environment.

Remember, you only get one chance at life. There's no going back. It's not like acting in a film where you can change the script and re-record the scenes; it's more like a live performance that's happening and you get one take on each scene, each day moving closer to your last day on earth. I hope you're not wasting a second along the way doing things you'd rather not for the purpose of bringing profit and wealth to others, or for that matter in the pursuit of something that is unlikely to bring personal happiness to you.

Evaluate your daily activities and workplace and make each scene in your life happen the way you want without kowtowing to an institution intent on exploiting you for their own benefits.

Finally, don't misinterpret these thoughts as suggesting you shouldn't have wealth or material goods. The purpose is for you to do what makes you happy, in some cases that may result in both wealth and material goods, which won't likely make you happy unless you're attaining them by means that bring peace, happiness and goodwill to you and those who work for you.

In any case, such a scenario is unlikely to happen in a corporation, as your role there is to make someone else wealthy.

CHAPTER 10 – WHY ARE THEY SO HAPPY?

With the formation of the World Happiness Index by the United Nations in 2011, a World Happiness Report has been released every year since 2012.

In 2023 the top seven countries were listed for 2021 in order of rank as Finland, Denmark, Switzerland, Iceland, Netherlands, Norway, and Sweden.[12]

An honorable mention went to Bhutan, who was excluded in 2021 due to a technicality, which as near as I could tell, resulted from a lack of polling data due to the Covid-19 pandemic because they were included in earlier reports.

The honorable mention award to Bhutan prompted me to look at previous reports, and in particular the 2019 World Happiness Report, that averaged three years of data from 2016-2018.

At this point, the mystery grew. Bhutan ranked 95th on the U.N.'s happiness scale. It seemed unlikely that it would suddenly rank as an honorable mention behind the top seven countries in the 2022 report.

A closer look yields some interesting information. The first is that the whole concept of a "Happiness Index" began in Bhutan in 1972 when the King declared "Gross National Happiness is more important than Gross Domestic Product."[13]

At that time the government of Bhutan decided that all decisions in the government would consider the impact on the happiness and welfare of the people, and when tensions were observed between economic development and happiness and peace, preference would be given to happiness and peace. Overall, Bhutan is known to be one of the happiest populations in the world—so why the discrepancy and the ranking of 95th in the world?

The Index included the following domains: [13]

1. Psychological wellbeing
2. Health
3. Education
4. Time use
5. Cultural diversity and resilience
6. Good governance
7. Community vitality
8. Ecological diversity and resilience
9. Living standards

Since that time, in Bhutan, 33 indicators have been added into the nine domains with the goal of helping create policy that will lead to increased happiness in the society.

While this whole notion of a "Gross National Happiness Index" started in Bhutan in 1972, in 2011, the UN unanimously adopted a General Assembly resolution, introduced by Bhutan with support from 68 member states, calling for a "holistic approach to development" aimed at promoting sustainable happiness and wellbeing.

Let's stop and consider this notion, because for most governments, or private developers in the world, the phrase "holistic approach to development" in order to provide happiness and well-being, is a foreign thought, or at the very least subject to an interpretation that must include profits for someone.

The following information defines most succinctly Bhutan's concept for guiding their nation. I recommend reading the entire paper entitled *An extensive analysis of the GNH Index*, [14]

The Fifth King, His Majesty Jigme Khesar Namgyel Wangchuck described Gross National Happiness or GNH as a more holistic approach requiring addressing the wellbeing of both current and future generations, while achieving an equitable level of wellbeing for the people.

There was a focus on allowing people to prioritize happiness in sustainable ways, and such that it would be seen as a common public good.

Perhaps the more profound definition of happiness includes the separation of happiness from pleasure, and feel-good type moods brought by the possession of material goods and wealth.

Additionally, the idea included that true happiness comes from serving others and living in harmony with nature. This harmony with nature is perhaps one of the primary factors that has been lost in the pursuit of wealth without regard to the sustainability of the pursuit.

For the western mind, it's perhaps unthinkable that happiness could be more important than Gross Domestic Product. **Imagine if a company used this approach in their business**. I need to clarify what I mean when I refer to the "western mind" because recently, China and other countries have joined the capitalistic pursuit, or race for technology and wealth, so I would offer that my definition of western mind may refer more to a value system with respect to money and wealth than a region or particular government, as may have been generalized in the past.

When I think about just how far from our Westernized concepts of corporate productivity and expectations Bhutan's belief system is, it makes me sad, but at the same time gives me perspective as to why our population is unhappy as a whole.

Picture Elon Musk telling his employees that only exceptional performance will warrant keeping their jobs, or the robot systems monitoring the employees on the Amazon production line to move product faster. Is there any personal concern for humanity? It leads one to wonder what the point of living is.

I saw a video with, Kevin O'Leary, "Mr. Wonderful" from the Shark Tank saying something to the affect that any *quiet-quitter* wouldn't be working for him.[15] The real problem with many of these individuals that expect the work-force to feed their economic and egotistical needs isn't the fact that they are ego driven, but the fact that they are so lost in a value system that is unlikely to ever bring happiness to them or anyone around them.

They are often driven by other factors which are also inherent in human nature, including both power and money, by definition the two most venal characteristics humans carry.

The larger problem is that many organizations feel it is necessary to exploit workers, or essentially take more from them than they give back in order to gain profit.

"O'Leary himself says he looks to hire people who are willing to put in '25 hours a day, eight days a week'"[15]. In the large institutions, this certainly does not come with long-term gains, though it might in a smaller company where one's effort is more likely to be recognized.

As for O'Leary, only he knows his intentions, but he may have misunderstood the benefits of *quiet-quitting* in a large corporation.

Beyond showing profits, the publicly traded institutions have but one goal. Their goal is to grow. By definition, growth will always be finite, and at the very least the rate of growth will have to slow down at some point, so their long-term goal is destined to fail. It's just a question of when.

Thus, by definition, in the western corporate approach, humanity is not able to pursue human well-being in a sustainable manner. And I suppose that does beg the question as to whether or not human well-being has any relevance in the overall scope of the world. This book argues that it does!

Should slowed growth or no growth necessarily lead to the demise of a publicly traded company? Perhaps the problem is the idea of a publicly traded company to begin with, given that their value is rarely based on assets, but rather projections and speculation.

Perhaps the saddest part of all of this is that the Western Society has nearly lost touch with the idea that happiness is not totally controlled by socioeconomics, GDP, GNP, and wealth.

While our minds can process that Bhutan is a happy culture, and even give them an honorable mention for happiness, notably absent is any discussion of how this condescending pat on the back connects them with the current economic factors on the measuring stick that places them 95th in the world, hardly in the top ten on the happiness scale, and hardly the view the Bhutanese have of their own happiness.

The resolution of this discrepancy may lie in the fact that the World Happiness Council of the UN that was inspired by Bhutan, places heavier emphasis on socio-economic factors such as Income Level, GDP, healthcare systems, etc.

The truth is, by weighting the variables in the statistical analysis to whatever value system one has, any desired country could be placed at the top. This is one of the dangers of developing an arbitrary statistical model.

It's convenient and seems reasonable to place in high regard factors in measuring happiness such as the quality of the healthcare system, affordability of education, along with GDP and poverty levels.

But there's an inclination to question the statistical weighted concept of happiness when one considers that in Finland, who is ranked number 1 for happiness based on these and other socio-economic factors, the suicide rate is 300% higher than in Bhutan[16] whereas the median income in Bhutan is more than 650% lower than in Finland. [17]

Unfortunately, it's not only Finland, but all of the top-ranking "happiness" countries have a much higher suicide rate than Bhutan.

Again, perhaps our Western definition of a happiness index is mis-guided. Is it possible that it's not in our reality or mindset to remove the concept of wealth and money from a happiness scale? From our deepest roots, we correlate wealth with happiness.

As material wealth has grown well beyond the basic means required for comfort, we've continued to equate higher levels of wealth with increased happiness, and we've witnessed governments declaring certain levels of wealth as an entitlement in order to bring those who have not attained it more happiness at the expense of those who have.

Or.... Perhaps because our institutions are so focused on productivity for the sake of making money this notion of a Happiness Index has been distorted for political or philosophical purposes not necessarily related to the humans' actual contentment with the life they were given.

Or... perhaps our cultures have increased our sense of entitlement of wealth to the point that even when we have it handed to us, we still want to go kill ourselves when faced with minimal adversity because as individuals we have lost the tools or mental fortitude to navigate the true challenges of human existence independently.

These are not simple questions nor have they simple answers, but it's safe to assume that anytime a group of people begin defining subjective matters, it's likely to be biased towards the personal values of the cultures involved or to meet the goals of those hoping to direct a society. It only becomes dangerous when it's presented as a science to promote a certain type of government or value system.

Drug-related deaths in Finland have doubled in the last twenty years, with the proportion of deaths of people under the age of 30 rising from 33% to 49%.

For men under the age of 40 in Finland, the most common cause of death – after suicide – is overdose. This year, those caught driving under the influence of drugs exceeded the number of drivers under the influence of alcohol.[18]

With all that said, I would re-iterate that factors determining happiness are culturally oriented, and publishing and ranking countries happiness levels may be biased towards the desired outcome of the agency presenting the data.

CHAPTER 11 – WHY NOT CHOOSE HAPPINESS?

One of the problems that has developed in the evolution of our society appears to be a confusion of what happiness is, and what brings happiness. Given the number of studies that have been carried out, and the known results, it's surprising that we still seem to lack an understanding.

Many people confuse pleasure with happiness. While it may be pleasurable to have a massage, or have sex, or listen to good music, or party, dance, use drugs, get inebriated, etc., pleasure really has nothing to do with happiness. There are many very unhappy people who spend a lot of their time participating in pleasurable activities. Happiness and pleasure don't seem to correlate.

In most western societies, wealth is seen as another means to happiness, even though studies on the subject seem to suggest this is not true. Money definitely buys pleasure, but this adds to the confusion of defining happiness.

We are constantly bombarded by the media with what wealth might bring us, from expensive vacations to large houses and cars. We are taught to envy wealth and with this envy comes the belief, or at least the feeling, that more wealth will bring more happiness. We buy our lottery tickets and watch the drawing in anticipation, hoping to be the one in a million who gets to be happy.

Yet, we have continuous examples of wealthy people who are very unhappy, commit suicide, overdose on drugs, are unable to carry on lasting relationships, and whose children are equally unhappy. The fact that there are a lot of unhappy wealthy people doesn't mean wealthy people can't be happy. I expect they have about the same ratio of happiness as the general population.

Given that we know money is not the key to happiness, we have to ask ourselves why we're willing to forfeit our happiness to slave in a job when we believe it might result in more money.

AN ALTERNATE VALUE SYSTEM

For a moment, let's shift gears from "Western World" happiness definitions to "Eastern World" thought, and in particular back to the country of Bhutan, where all national policy is premised on bringing happiness to the citizens. The median annual income in Bhutan is less than $2500.00 per year. [17] The happiness value placed on wealth is essentially non-existent.

While this is not an exploration of religion, Bhutan is largely driven by Buddhist principles and a brief consideration of Buddhism might serve to better understand the difference in the happiness index.

In the West, it seems many churches have perverted the basic message of Christianity and now there are churches that preach the prosperity doctrine, which allows that living the Christian life will result in financial rewards.

We see televangelists riding in chauffer driven Rolls Royces, flying in private jets, and professing their lifestyle as an attestation of God's reward for their good work while they bombard us for donations with 1-800 numbers from behind the walls of their tax shelters.

Even more experienced at the game of wealth, the Vatican hoards money while requiring a vow of poverty from priests and nuns.

The Mormon Church has defined complex heavenly social classes with the materialistic standards of living defined by their service and monetary contributions to their church while alive on earth. They were also recently fined 5 million dollars for using shell companies to obscure the size of a portfolio under church control. [19]

This justification of the quest for wealth and power on earth in the name of God seems a gross bastardization of Christ's teachings by the organizations who stand to gain from this exploitation of humanity's weaknesses in much the same way corporations do. In fact, the correlation between wealth and religion does not seem to exist statistically, and such a discussion might be used (and probably has been used) to justify violent criminal activity. Are the Mexican drug cartels being rewarded with the billions of dollars because of their religion? Are the billionaire Russian Oligarchs who pillaged wealth upon the collapse of the Soviet Union being rewarded for their religion?

The simple message in Corinthians 13:13 and presented throughout the New Testament: "And now abide faith, hope, love, these three; but the greatest of these is love" seems to have been lost by many masquerading as teachers of the Christian word as a means to gain wealth.

The one belief that seems to have evolved over time in western society, religious or not, is the idea that more wealth and material goods bring more happiness.

The purpose of this book though, is not to suggest that there is anything wrong with wealth or religion. Rather, an understanding that wealth does not bring happiness is a message that would serve us well in that it might change how we treat our fellow humans as we seek it.

Buddhism on the other hand is defined by the Four Noble Truths, and an eightfold path as to how to live life. While it's open to debate if this happiness in Bhutan is due to their religion or some other reason, not only has the focus of Buddhism and its associated institutions never shifted towards money as a reward for good deeds, but it maintains that happiness is found in a whole different realm.

The Four Noble Truths of Buddhism[20] (in their simplest form):

1.) The truth of suffering: Life is suffering.

2.) The truth of the cause of suffering: The cause of suffering is desire or craving.

3.) The truth of the end of suffering: The end of suffering comes with the end of craving or desire.

4.) The truth of the path that frees us from suffering: There is a path which leads one away from craving and thus, suffering.

Buddhist teachings point out that the cause of suffering is emotions. In particular, the emotion of desiring and craving. Examples might be craving more wealth, more material goods, and/or the fear of loss. At its core, Buddhism teaches that everything, including these emotions, is impermanent so attachment is fruitless and only leads to suffering.

The eightfold path of Buddhism is meant to lead one to detachment from the cravings, and the clinging with the ultimate goal being to end suffering through acceptance of the impermanence of everything.

We can see that the Buddhist idea of happiness is much different than the western world, for happiness does not revolve around material wealth or seeking more wealth. *In fact, it suggests that the craving for more is a root cause of suffering and unhappiness in humans*.

It is important to understand that according to Buddhism, it's not wealth, or possession of material goods that lead to unhappiness, it's the attachment to these items, the craving for more, and the belief that they will bring happiness.

Understanding that your life, your family, your health, and if you have it, your wealth, along with happiness, and sadness are all temporary states of being that do not last help one place these cravings in their proper perspective. In Buddhism the impermanence of our Physical state of being is taught. Christianity at its core teaches that none of this belongs to us, it belongs to a God, whereas Buddhism suggests we are all just a part of the Universe whether living or dead. Both are saying the same thing with respect to attachment to worldly matters, but somewhere along the line large facets of Christianity devoted themselves to the attainment of wealth whereas Buddhism has not.

The eightfold path is a prescription for living that is said to cure these cravings. The eight areas addressed are: Right View, Right Resolve, Right Speech, Right Action, Right Livelihood, Right Effort, Right Mindfulness, and Right Concentration. It's notable that "Right Livelihood", or "Work" is included.

In the West, our entire value system revolves around trying to satisfy these cravings through consumption and the gaining of wealth, while in the Buddhist system, it's believed the cure to all of man's suffering is to accept that none of this has any real significance or adds value to one's life, and understanding this stops the cravings.

It's the attachment and the craving that is the problem. Regardless of whether one even considers religion, if one considers all the crazy things people do in order to gain, or for that matter, hang onto wealth, the problem becomes more evident.

People (and companies) will lie, cheat, steal, kill, betray family and friends, and abuse the trust of acquaintances to gain and maintain wealth. If we examine an entity such as a business and remove ethics and morals, the only thing that stops them from carrying out certain activities is fear of the consequences of getting caught. Unfortunately, such a system is begging for sociopathic leaders and such personality types are most likely to succeed in this environment.

The real question is: *Is this something you want to participate in?* By the way, I'm not suggesting that all companies are run like this, but I am suggesting that ultimately, when push comes to shove, all publicly traded companies and many private companies place increased profits and income above all else to the point that most readers of this text can't even fathom how another business model might succeed.

Even that in and of itself is not bad, because I think everyone can agree that if a company does not make money, it will cease to exist.

What's being called into question is if by changing priorities of what the company stands for, perhaps life could be better for everyone, thereby increasing not only the quality of life of those employed, but also the long-term chance of survival of the company.

For example: Let's say that a company defined its employees happiness as its number one priority, and making more money as its second priority.

This would be a game changer. This is actually what psychological advisers are telling companies to do. It's not advice they are likely to follow because with the current system's focus on short term profits, it would place their existence at risk.

In order to exist, people have to keep giving (investing) publicly traded companies more money so they can buy more stuff and increase their net worth. Remember, invested money is not borrowed money, it's just money given by investors for the perceived value of a company at any given time. The investment is based on the hopes and beliefs that the company will have greater value in the future.

For stocks to go up in value, the company has to grow, or at least people have to believe it's going to grow. Without that people would stop giving them money.

The CEOs get paid unbelievable salaries to perform this illusory magic. That is, until they can't maintain the illusion any longer; then the stocks tank, and everyone loses everything, except those who knew to sell the stock short. Examples might be J.C. Penney's, or Sears, or K-mart who were once great companies, but now exist as nearly zero value holding companies.

A company could, and many do, reduce the pressures on their work force. Unfortunately, most of them resort to laying people off as a first move in any downturn as this cost cutting helps the company maintain the illusion of profits, which helps keep the stock price up.

Likewise, it's very rare that the CEO and upper management take cuts in salary until long after the lower wage workers jobs have been sacrificed, and the stock's manipulated so that the upper crust can profit from the loss by selling short or unloading their personal stock prior to the price reductions.

Why have the millennials protested this? I think the obvious reason is because it all adds up to a form of looting. And as difficult as it is to change one's priorities, the only answer if working in one of these types of companies is to completely quit, or *quiet-quit*, because they are NEVER going to set up a fair playing field for most of their workforce; needless to say, the principles and values of their leaders go completely against everything that is known with regards to long term sustainability.

CHAPTER 12 – WHY *QUIET-QUIT*?

The simple truth is, and it's well established—more money, more material goods, and more debt, does not bring more happiness. A bigger house and exotic car may satisfy the ego, but ego is not related to happiness.

In our world, we have somehow come to think that our boss is happier than we are, and getting that promotion will make us happier. The problem is, in order to get to that position and help create that illusion, our boss likely had to appear to have more than she/he had by indebting herself/himself to the bank to finance a lifestyle, which in turn placed the corporate handcuffs on her/him until the corporation is ready to unlock her/him and send her/him into oblivion.

Trust me, it's unlikely that she or he is happier than you are if working in a large corporation.

Perhaps the real truth is that the corporate ladder is intentionally set up so that you can, at best, inch towards your materialistic and wealth-oriented goals. The one thing you will never attain in a corporation is independence so if that's something you need, it's a real mistake to be on the corporate ladder.

I'll never forget an experience I had as a young Engineer when one of our division heads, I'll call him William, built a new home. At the time I was in my mid-twenties, and I suspect he was around fifty. He had recently been promoted to "Division-Head" which was somewhere on the upper end of mid-management on the corporate ladder. With his promotion came a raise.

He invited everyone to the new home he built following his promotion. It was finely staged by a professional and was in an upper middle-class neighborhood with a peek-a-boo view of the Puget Sound. Everyone oohed and awed at the housewarming party and were amazed that one could have the wealth for such an upscale home. As a new graduate, I was excited that I might live such a lifestyle in thirty years. It certainly encouraged us all to stay on the corporate ladder.

Unfortunately, the wind shifted in our industry a few months later, and layoffs ensued. It seemed the fifty-year olds were more expensive labor in general, and William lost his job along with a lot of other folks around his age. I was assured my job was not at risk. Soon after, when William lost his house, it became clear that his success was an illusion created by a salary that allowed taking out a large mortgage at 50+ years old.

Thank you, lesson learned. The illusion was burst, and if it bursts at the wrong point in life, as in the case of William, there is nowhere left to go. I was lucky to experience this at the beginning of my career.

In fact, given what's been shown about the psychology of management in a large corporation, for most, independence, happiness, and wealth are very unlikely. True happiness might come in a self-employed world even with a much lower income, but in truth there is likely a higher probability of income as well.

Another strong motivator to *quiet-quit* is the fact that many people want their family to be an integral part of their lives. With today's corporations view that any energy placed by an employee elsewhere equates to lost profits, this is very difficult. Whether your reason for *quiet-quitting* is to seek alternate employment, or to improve your quality of life at home it will likely help you reach your goals.

As I mentioned earlier, this book is not directed at those who are attaining a life of fulfillment working in a corporation, but rather to encourage those who don't feel they are reaching their true potential in such an environment to seek alternatives.

I was one of those early in my career. Around thirty-five years ago my first step towards independence began with what is now called *quiet-quitting*. It took about four years of planning along with obtaining another degree while working "quietly" before I was able to venture on my own.

Thankfully, I wasted a bare minimum of my energy on the corporation that I worked in. If you feel you're wasting your time, the question is how much time are you willing to waste during this single exploration of life that you have?

Chapter 13 – A Complete Reset

If you've found that any of this makes sense, I believe we're ready to look a bit deeper into the root of the problem.

The Real Problem

The real problem in our society is not capitalism, materialism, or monetary wealth, **it's that we use wealth to place a value on human beings in general**. As a whole, our society places much higher values on humans who are wealthy or famous, which often goes hand in hand. Unfortunately, this may be true in most societies.

We feel because they're wealthier, their lives also have more value. While it's not uncommon for wealthy people to feel this way about themselves with respect to those with less wealth, the exoneration of the wealthy by those with less wealth is the real surprise and seems to be more a product of a society that covets wealth over almost everything else.

In essence, because of their wealth, our society grants them privileges that we don't allow those who do not have monetary wealth, and we forgive them for breaking many rules that most of us would never think of breaking. In fact, we don't expect to have the same privileges they have as we don't see ourselves as worthy, until, or unless we carry that same wealth. Often, we are simply envious of them.

With social media we can link into their accounts and hear from them daily as if they're our best friends, so it's only getting worse. Funny, we rarely consider that they have no clue who we are, nor do they know anything about our lives while we focus on knowing as much as possible about theirs.

When we learned Tiger Woods was screwing numerous escorts, his fans shrugged and thought, that's what rich people do, then forgave him. When Donald Trump talked about grabbing them by the pussy his supporters forgave him. When Mick Jagger cheated on every girlfriend or wife he had - over and over, rock fans didn't bat an eyelid because he's a rock star. Isn't that what they're supposed to do?

When Bill Clinton *didn't* have sexual relations with that girl, but he really *did*, his own lack of shame and sense of privilege and entitlement allowed him to hold his head high and fight to remain in office, while most of us would be so ashamed we would never want to be seen in public again. Yet, for him, we excused it.

This isn't to say that those close to these people weren't hurt, or in some cases destroyed, it's just that we weren't concerned about those who were hurt, for our hopes and dreams lie with our privileged heroes.

When someone we admire is rich or famous, we see them on an elevated platform, and we want them to stay there so we excuse behaviors that might knock them off it. In fact, in some cases we willingly propagate stories we know to be untrue to protect them. If it's someone we don't admire; then we wonder why they get away with everything. Donald Trump has probably proved this more than any other well-known person in history.

The same was true in the 2009 Housing Crash, when millions of people lost their homes. While the government didn't bail any of these unfortunate individuals out, and as a society we had little sympathy for them, it was the risk free, government backed, predatory loans with variable APR that led to this crisis.

It was the criminal behavior of the lenders, and their withholding of information and lying to the public about their financial state that led to the crash and destroyed thousands of lives. But how many went to jail? No, we excuse them. In fact, because the web of lies was so deep that our economy was at risk, we allowed congress to raise our taxes to pay for their lies, and we excused Congress as well.

I suppose, the fact that it was a collusion between government and business could excuse the fact that the government bailed all these companies out while ignoring the individuals whose lives were destroyed, but the real questions is; why wasn't the public outraged?

After all, it was the middle-class taxpayer who paid to bail these banks and corporations out, and the middle-class who paid the taxes to cover these guaranteed loans such that the banks could walk away from them at no cost, no penalty, and no responsibility.

Again, apparently, we've been so conditioned to accept that those rich entities are entitled that our deserved outrage is subdued. More recently, everyone has been trained to blame _the other_ political party for anything that goes wrong. Is it possible that this partisan hatred we're being conditioned to participate in is an intentional diversion to prevent us from seeing what's really going on, a way to keep our anger focused away from the real problems, and those responsible?

So, what's the point?

THE FIRST POINT IS THIS

Our society admires and craves wealth. We think the wealthy have a better life, we seem to think they deserve a better life, and we excuse them for not living up to universal moral and ethical values that most of us require of ourselves. We excuse them for gaining their wealth in ways we would never consider doing. A problem with having wealth is that there is never enough so one only craves more.

Corporations dangle the carrot and allow their employees to nibble on that lifestyle to create the illusion that the employee might obtain that better life. The threat of losing it encourages the managers and administrators to participate in the lies told by the corporations.

THE SECOND POINT IS THIS

The idea that having more of everything brings more happiness is 180 degrees different than the tenets of Buddhism, which state that it is the desire for more that leads to suffering and misery.

"**Nirvana is the state of liberation from our desires, cravings, and attachments.** It is not something that happens overnight, but rather it is something that can be achieved through following the Eightfold Path." [21]

Considering that an entire philosophy for living happily is founded on the above statement, and it's the exact opposite of the belief that consuming and gaining wealth will bring happiness, I believe it warrants more discussion.

If we look at the metrics for the happiness index in the Global Happiness ratings since 2012 when the U.N. took Bhutan's idea, we find that it was "westernized" by weighting heavier measures of wealth and material comforts in the statistical model. While it's noble to work towards higher standards of living for a population, the truth is, it's proven that beyond meeting basic human needs for comfortable survival, it doesn't create a happier society.

Given that the entire precept of the corporation is to gain wealth and profit, and often through deception, and lying, the level of misguidance is overwhelming, at least with respect to bringing anyone employed in such an organization happiness in life.

An example would be the giant bank Wells Fargo who has repeatedly broken laws and destroyed people's lives with their predatory policies and corporate greed. Through pressure for profit, they created a culture that led to creative lies by their staff and resulted in large amounts of well documented fraud.

Though they have been repeatedly fined, most recently 3.7 billion dollars, they fail to change their behavior.

"Put simply: Wells Fargo is a corporate recidivist that puts one out of three Americans at risk for potential harm," said CFPB Director Rohit Chopra, in a call with reporters."[22] Note: the CFPB or Consumer Financial Protection Bureau is the agency that has levied these fines on Wells Fargo.

Why isn't the public outraged? How does Wells Fargo continue to exist and profit at the public's expense? Who still does business with these crooks? Simply put, we allow it, and the government allows it.

When one stops and considers the depths these corporations go to, and the level they push their employees to in order to deceive the public, is it any surprise that the millennials have called time out? Would you like to devote your life to working in a company like this?

Though there are numerous examples, I believe the next one is so egregious that it cannot be glossed over. I'm talking about the Boeing 737 MAX debacle. Following the investigation, Boeing admitted that they defrauded the FAA to get the plane certified by not disclosing the safety issues that they knew existed.

Still, after having the ruling overturned to pave the way for potential prosecution, they entered a plea of not guilty to felony fraud. Three hundred and forty-six people died in these crashes. These crashes occurred because Boeing wanted the plane in production and had cut corners to save money. They admitted to lying to the government in order to get the plane certified. If the government had not finally grounded the planes there would likely have been more deaths.

Following the crash, the CEO was fired. As if he was the one that made the decision, and this would cure the problem. Imagine some poor schmuck who pleads guilty to simple manslaughter and gets sentenced to 11 years in prison. (drunk driving for example. Wait... I believe that drunk driving is now considered murder so prison time might be much longer.)

Yet.... A large corporation kills 346 humans because they're too cheap to get the job done right and know full well they are risking lives. A CEO gets fired, everyone points fingers to somewhere else, the company pays fines, and the company apologizes, stating how bad they feel for the families. My question: Who's going to jail? The answer: Nobody.

And we ask—How can this be? The answer: Because we allow it, our government allows it. Again, it's the privilege and value we allow those who have wealth.

If not one, but all corporations reset their priorities in the following order, they would naturally be much more successful, have a happier and healthier workforce, and likely a more sustainable long term success story. Needless to say, the public's health and well-being would improve.

PRIORITIES IN ORDER OF IMPORTANCE:

  1.) Employees happiness and well-being.

  2.) Highest quality product and service.

  3.) Profits to company and owners.

One problem with the larger companies is that the management is rarely held accountable for their actions at an individual level in ways that might change the environment. Much like the internet provides anonymity, large corporations seem to shield individuals from responsibility. To change this behavior would require retraining from the ground up.

This is unlikely as larger companies continuously tilt the playing field by lobbying congress to pass legislation that make it very difficult to hold any individuals accountable.

Likewise, the legislation makes it increasingly difficult for small businesses to start or establish themselves unless they are funded from within the circle of wealth. The idea of stomping out the competition by creating rules that make it difficult for them, or cheating and lying for gains are not new. Unfortunately, it's very difficult to bring to light and generally takes years of court cases as the cheaters double down, not to mention they have more resources to fight off those trying to expose them.

One example is the tobacco industry's lying about the dangers of tobacco, and their attempts to get people addicted. A more recent case is that of Purdue Pharma who sold Oxycontin as a wonder drug with the full intention of addicting millions of people to create a steady revenue stream. Their actions played a large part in creating the opioid crisis and was deliberate.

A more recent example is the development of privacy laws in healthcare which are being used to prevent the reporting of fraudulent activity by employees. This is done by making it a prosecutable offense for the employee to retain any evidence of the fraud, effectively gagging the healthcare workers and rendering the chances of any prosecution null.[23]

Again, the problem with wealth is that there's never enough, and greed causes people, and companies to do terrible things without regard for human lives.

This book is not about changing the habits of corporations, it's about empowering the people who are working for these corporations to improve their own lives. The illness governing these corporations is such that it will take more than individuals to help them.

Quiet-quitting allows one to focus on alternatives while still making a living. It offers a way out to those who have not yet been engulfed in the flame of fear driven greed but are still working in such an environment. A chance to reclaim one's soul, if you will.

CHAPTER 14 – BUDDHISM IS NOT REQUIRED TO SUCCEED

As our world becomes more divided, we see extreme political views, each certain that their superior political philosophy will somehow make society better. We now see religions involving themselves in politics in the U.S. and using God as their justification. Unfortunately, there don't seem to be any political systems or religions that can demonstrate a clean record for the people they are chartered to serve.

Power may be the real corruptor because the downfalls seem to begin immediately when a new government has replaced the previous corrupt government. This is equally true in publicly traded corporations where leadership is governed by politics.

A consistent constant is that once an institution is well established and carries a certain amount of wealth and power, being in charge of that entity more often than not leads to some level of corruption. Often the corruption is required prior to attaining the leadership position.

To determine root cause is somewhat of a chicken or egg question. Because money is a necessary precursor to attaining those powerful positions, people go to great lengths to obtain money. The truth is, no political system will reduce this human quest for wealth and power. The question is whether or not there is a way to organize the pursuit in a humane fashion.

THE THREE POISONS IN BUDDHISM

1.) *Greed*

2.) *Hatred*

3.) *Delusion*

Is it possible that these three poisons are responsible for many of the problems in the world today?

Consider the fact that Greed is used as one of the factors to argue against capitalism, yet, capitalism has brought the world innovation, technology, and many solutions to world problems, and human health. The Western Nations have led in all aspects of technology only to be copied and followed by lesser developed countries. The Western Nations tend to be Capitalistic.

Greed becomes a problem in any situation where power is gained and access to wealth and material goods goes untethered. We see this in every political system, so singling out capitalism as a culprit carries very little weight, especially after a close examination of the political leaders of all forms of government.

While greed is a root problem of many corporations, rather than being a problem of capitalism, it appears to be a flaw of human nature that has exhibited its dangers equally in various governments as free market economies.

From the standpoint that each of us are trying to improve our own lives and living condition, I would suggest that capitalism is somewhat inherent in human nature, but does not necessarily facilitate or require greed.

Hatred is something that seems to be escalating throughout the world, and though this is not something new, google algorithms, social media, and the anonymity the internet allows, seem to have brought it to new heights. Likewise, hatred is pushed by political organizations. The reason for this isn't clear but appears to be a deliberate attempt to direct the blame for society's problems to alternate political belief systems, rather than the political and corporate collusion that is draining the middle class.

There was a time not so long ago when two people with different political beliefs could disagree without having to hate each other. In truth, simply understanding that most of our beliefs come from the life we have lived should make it acceptable that others would have different beliefs. We have not all lived the same lives in the same environment.

Our governments and corporations both stand to benefit from having us hate any entity that threatens their well-being. Remember though, they are the ones who benefit from the hatred they instill in us, we don't.

Delusion is perhaps the easiest state to live in and probably the most damaging to humanity. (Recall the followers of Hitler). Unfortunately, the practice of placing their employees into a delusional state is a well-researched and well-plotted activity of large corporations.

The problem with this approach is that when reality is not faced for any reason, denial, ignorance, etc., the damage only compounds.

The situations where CEOs earning multi millions per year stand in a court or in front of Congress and lie are examples where society has to some extent licensed the corporations to live in a delusional world. I say we have licensed them, because we allow them the delusion that they are privileged and therefore allowed criminal activity.

Further examples of this would be in corporations that deny the damage they are doing to the environment, or the devastating effects their narcotics are having on human lives, or more recently, the injection of addictive unhealthy foods into the daily diet of the population.

When combined with greed, delusion can lead to a medical system as it now exists in the United States where profit outweighs all decisions of healthcare. The delusion that corporate profits in Health Insurance and Big Pharma, outweigh any value of wellness of human beings is perhaps the epitome of where these three poisons can lead, and the United States is leading the world in showing how this can destroy a health care system.

I'm sure each of you can think of more examples, though it's uncomfortable for most of us to face this harsh reality and denial is a more comfortable state.

In Buddhism, they claim three antidotes to the three poisons, though I would suggest that the antidotes are really a **prescription for happiness** on an individual level, and a **prescription for success** on a Corporate level.

ANTIDOTE TO THE THREE POISONS.

   1.) Generosity

   2.) Lovingkindness

   3.) Wisdom

Generosity comes in many forms, but in all forms, caring about yourself, your environment, other humans, and the future of mankind are where it starts.

Greed is based on selfish care, and selfish care is what has poisoned many of these large corporations.

Lovingkindness is self-explanatory. Ask yourself if you feel that your corporation bases its activities around lovingkindness towards the world, the environment, its employees, and its customers.

Wisdom is possibly the only antidote to delusion, and unfortunately most only gain it when their current attempts at life or business are failing or have completely failed. This seems to be true of corporations as well. Most who choose to live in denial never learn it, and most individuals who have accepted their place in a corporation, or unhealthy situation, have moved to a state of pathological delusion.

Because many governments and corporations have vast amounts of resources, once they have taken the wrong path, wisdom is rarely necessary for survival in the short run due to the resources they have in place and the self-protective rules they have implemented on the playing field, which most often includes abusing their workforce.

The problem is that while we live in the short run, the long run is still coming. Because humans only live for 100 years or so, most of us consider 100 years the long run. In fact, the true long run is much longer if considerations are to be given to the planet, the environment, and the future generations of humans.

In the case of corporations, their life span is at risk continuously, and from the standpoint of those in charge every quarter (every 3 months) matters for their personal career and income. Wisdom is not even on the table, nor is it necessary for an organization's short-term survival once the resources are in place.

Much more important are creative accounting techniques to create an illusion of profits each quarter. Because of this, we often see what appears to be a strong company suffer a rapid collapse when the illusion cannot be maintained.

Because of the immense pressure on corporations to perform in short term windows, and the lies, greed, denial, and delusion required to do that, it is unlikely that they will change.

In fact, it's up to the employees, shareholders, and unfortunately, the government who has proven itself unreliable, to help these institutions reset their compasses.

As individuals, our tools are limited, and rather than chastise, we should commend the generation that started this process of *quiet-quitting* as it is a peaceful form of protest. As they age and take their positions of power, less and less of them will advocate, but with some luck, the movement can be passed on before it is too late.

Though *quiet-quitting* may seem trivial, there is strength in numbers and with continued presence in social media, it may have a positive effect on our society if it's not selfishly driven.

CHAPTER 15 – FINDING INSPIRATION IN TODAY'S WORLD

We must be realistic about both our place in the world, and the society we live in.

First, while the human quest for power, dominance, wealth, etc. is not going away, nor is the fact that only a small number of humans seeking the above will receive the winning lottery tickets either through birth rights, luck, talent, or force, there is solace in the fact that a large portion of the world's population are realizing that power and materialism are an unlikely road to happiness.

How do we find our path without being just a pawn in the game to bring wealth to those caught up in this mindset?

Given that we must navigate this reality as such, the **first step is to remove all denial about how many of these corporations are operating without morals or ethics, lest you be caught in their web.**

Consider Amazon and the workers conditions, Starbucks and their fight against unionization while their CEO sees huge raises, Wells Fargo and the continued fines, Big Pharma and the cost of drugs, Boeing and their disregard for human life—and the list never ends.

The fact is, they know what they are doing, and they know that it's wrong. It's just that they don't care, and they've gained enough power in the market, as well as influence in the government that they can say "F--- you if you don't like it" to the general population.

We also know what these companies are, and the first step towards finding inspiration is to accept that we can't change the ones that allow greed to control their actions. The important step is for you to decide who you are and what role you want to play in this world.

Ask yourself if you want your life to be devoted to helping such organizations flourish, and if you will be able to find lifelong ***motivation*** in this.

Does your company operate on the basis of the three poisons—Greed, Hatred, and Delusion?

Will their Modus Operandi create your life's legacy?

The litmus test is whether or not any one of these qualities have been demonstrated by your place of employment.

SEPARATING THE GOOD FROM THE BAD

Now realize that there are also many companies that operate without Greed, Hatred, and Delusion and do not use unethical tactics to create an illusion for their employees and shareholders.

Unfortunately, it's not so easy to tell which companies these are by their outward appearance or advertisements, or which charities they support, because some of the worst companies are the best imposters.

The answer lies in carrying out some research:

1.) *How often does the company have layoffs. (In fact, a company should rarely if ever require layoffs, even in the case of a major recession)*

2.) *What is the salary of their CEO in relationship to the average salary in the company?*

3.) *What do online surveys of employees say about the company you are researching?*

4.) *What is the annual employee turnover in the company? (Some companies shoot for a specified turnover rate to know that they are pushing their employees hard enough)*

Ask yourself how your current place of employment lines up with respect to the above metrics. If you find that when push comes to shove, you know you don't want to create your life's legacy in your current place of employment, it's time to consider an exit plan.

Depending on your financial needs, this may be via *quiet-quitting*, or if you have the means, simply quitting and starting your own business.

As a product of the University of Washington, student loans, and all of the indoctrination that goes with it, I can attest that letting go of years of training and much of what one was taught can be daunting, especially when there is no clear soft landing. I can also attest from personal experience that it is possible, and that with a realistic and practical approach, greater job satisfaction and financial success is likely.

In today's world of online businesses, and with numerous platforms to present new services or products, the opportunities for entrepreneurism are greater than at any time in history.

In order to pursue this path, the corporation must not be valued any more than they value you, which is a short-term means to reach their long-term goals. For you, it might be thought of as a short-term stopping point to reach your long-term goals. Thus, one should expend the minimum amount of energy required to keep a job and direct most energy towards developing an independent means of income.

Indeed, what can be learned from the book "In Search of Excellence" is how to perform at extraordinary levels regardless of how ordinary one is, and the wisdom to be gained is simply this: <u>Let yourself be the beneficiary of that extraordinary performance</u>.

The winning ticket is to take everything learned in those motivational books and apply it towards reaching your own personal goals.

In other words, take all the research that teaches companies the psychology of how to maximize your energy output and apply it to yourself such that you will perform at an extraordinary level in life but keep that energy focused on your personal goals. Use your knowledge to prevent that excess energy to feed the profits of a predatorial employer.

While the corporation is seeking to monetize your energy, money may or may not be what lights your fire. Regardless of what you are seeking, you will have a better chance of reaping those rewards outside of a corporate environment.

In fact, you would likely be better off spending your extra time researching how to invest in stocks or real estate while self-employed. This would increase the long-term odds of financial success substantially over working in a corporation.

If you prefer to see some other aspect of mankind benefit from your energy, consider directing your efforts towards creating a company that would provide a service to meet those goals.

If you need an income, working for a corporation for a time is not a terrible idea if you employ the *quiet-quitting* approach and never indebt yourself such that you must rely on the company. This approach allows you to build your business while collecting a salary from the corporation. The only safe way to view these entities is as a means of potential profit for yourself while not concerning yourself with their issues other than at the minimum level. Don't be fooled.

CHAPTER 16 – NO SUBSTITUTE FOR HARD WORK

Anyone who has found success in their life knows nothing has or ever will replace hard work in the quest for success whether one is seeking financial success or some other reward.

The problem with many corporations, especially publicly traded ones is that they have created an environment that hard work won't bring success to the individual beyond an unfulfilled promise in the form of a carrot on a stick that never materializes. Worse yet, their psychological games and lack of empathy for their workforce can and have destroyed the lives of many individuals.

That being said, it's important to understand that if one chooses the *quiet-quitting* approach for alternate rewards, an enormous amount of work is required in order find one's way out of the corporate trap.

There are certain people who live to work. These people enjoy working, and often, work is their hobby. Some people might call them workaholics, but the negative connotations of that label don't really do them justice so I will label such a person a "work hobbyist". As a "work hobbyist" most of my life, I considered myself lucky that my hobby tended to bring monetary rewards.

Enjoying work can be a wonderful way to go through life, but like any hobby, for continued fulfillment, there needs to be some type of end reward for the activity. For mountain climbers, the end reward is the summit. For musicians, the reward is often an appreciative audience. The same is true for artists. In some cases, the rewards can be monetary.

Unfortunately, the worst place in the world for a "work hobbyist" to work is in a large corporation. The reason is that this person is most likely to be manipulated via the institutional psychological methods discussed earlier in this book. As life's responsibilities unfold, and the rewards remain limited, the person may feel trapped, and after not seeing rewards the "work hobbyist" is very likely to lose appreciation for what is likely not only her/his hobby, but also her/his greatest asset in life.

Alternatively, the person may be subject to the psychological manipulation to the point that it has a negative effect on her/his health. Surely, we've all heard about employees who worked their entire career, only to die within a year after retirement. Most of us don't want to be that person.

I believe the ideal candidates for *quiet-quitting* are the "work hobbyists", or "workaholics" as they are the employees who are: 1.) willing to work endlessly, 2.) due to their high productivity, most likely to be held in a "working position" and trapped into working for minimal reward.

The beauty of corporations is that if the "work hobbyist" views them as a resource with limitations, one can focus one's hard work and energy in places that might bring the desired rewards while profiting from their bureaucracy.

Thus, the ambitious person can be thankful that somewhere, sometime, years ago, some "work-hobbyist" like Bill Boeing or Henry Ford had an idea that was so revolutionary or great it created a company that grew into an institution that required a large number of employees.

The large institutions create well-defined ladders to keep workers inching forward all the way to retirement. At one time, this was a functional model, but in today's world where the goal has become to squeeze unrealistic amounts of productivity out of their employees, long careers with one company are rare. We now see people hopping from one job to another with the hopes of finding something tolerable.

The bigger problem is that over the years, the companies have become greedier and try to draw more profits from the workers by reducing benefits such as well-paid overtime, paid vacations, medical benefits, retirements, etc. etc.

With the loss of morals and ethics in the business world, the only people that will get ahead in most of these organizations are those willing to play a more political game, or be a part of the many illegal and fraudulent activities these companies carry out in order to increase profits.

Unfortunately, an individual will never (or rarely) win by trying to bring to light such activities, or attempting to correct them due to the unethical training of many of the company leaders, and the sociopathic breeding ground known as the MBA program.

In fact, that individual risks paying a very heavy price due to the overall criminal nature of the leadership of most of these large organizations. Many whistle blowers have paid these prices.

So, what's the point? The point about corporations has been well made throughout, but the goal of this chapter is to make it clear that if one opts to use quiet-quitting to get ahead the road to success will require even more hard work than putting up with corporate demands. While this may come natural for some, others may be surprised at how much work is required.

This work factor separates the winners from the losers because to come out ahead using *quiet-quitting* may require near super-human levels of effort. It is very difficult to find the energy required for anyone other than one who lives for work or at the least has a very focused vision of one's goals.

Another challenge is that corporations fight hard against the notion of *putting in an eight-hour day for eight-hours of pay* because of the fear that it could become a movement, and the only way to keep control of the workforce is to maintain a certain level of oppression.

One thing I've found in my life is that everyone thinks they are hard workers. The only people who see that others aren't working hard are those who work harder. Anyone who has owned and operated their own business understands this. Likewise, entrepreneurs know that the pot of gold may not be at the end of the rainbow regardless of how hard they work.

Thus, if you're only counting today's income, you're unlikely to ever make it in the world of *quiet-quitting.* Still, for those hard workers with financial responsibilities, there is no better place to maintain an income than a corporation while finding a more independent approach to life.

WHAT DOES HARD WORK MEAN?

The answer varies, but my answer is that it means to be working most of the time until you find the success you are after, whether it's monetary, or other. My own experience of *quiet-quitting* meant taking night classes for several years while working daily, and then, while starting my own business, working without any days off for several years while maintaining an income, and working on starting my own business.

Suffice it to say that it requires a lot of energy, and there's no way to sugar coat the competitiveness in the world. Out working the competition is one approach to success, but working smarter, not harder, may be just as important.

HARD WORK IS NOT ENOUGH.

Unfortunately, in today's world many people are being told they can succeed at whatever they want if they work hard enough.

This isn't true either. While hard work is a necessary ingredient, so too is finding someone who desires the work or product one offers.

Many years ago, I was told there are three and only three ingredients to success:

1.) The desire.

2.) The ability.

3.) The opportunity.

This statement is true, and unfortunately many people with desire and ability don't understand that one cannot create something that others don't want to pay for and still succeed in business. I think telling people that can succeed at whatever they want is great, but keeping food on the table in artistic endeavors such as music, writing, painting, etc. require an element of luck and timing so the "opportunity" is much more difficult to find and much more akin to buying a lottery ticket.

This is another reason to stay with the corporation in a quiet-quitting mode for those whose hearts lie in the arts.

WHEN TO QUIT COMPLETELY

As a side note, I would encourage anyone who works for a corporation that is or has been involved in activities one knows are illegal, morally or ethically wrong, or participates in customer deception, and false statements to simply quit and find another place of employment, regardless of how the company justifies these actions.

A close look at many large medical companies reveals a surprising number that have paid large fines for fraudulent activity, and many are on government "probation" type programs. My own experience with these companies has revealed that rather than slow or stop the fraud, it causes them to improve their methods of shifting that liability from the organization to the individual employees to reduce their own risk.

CHAPTER 17 – A SUMMARY OF QUIET-QUITTING

At this point, I'm hopeful you can see that *quiet-quitting* has nothing to do with lack of motivation, and everything to do with highly motivated individuals reclaiming their rights to benefit from their efforts vs having the results of their contributions directed towards shareholders profits and CEOs salaries.

The strong backlash and negative view of *quiet-quitting* being pushed by corporations and many employers is no surprise because much like unionization, or any form of worker protest, *quiet-quitting* is an effort to reduce the exploitation of the workforce, and if organized properly might actually succeed. No corporation wants that.

Perhaps some of the problem stems from the advanced state of evolution of capitalism combined with the advanced state of technology utilizing Artificial Intelligence, which while leading to a more efficient economy, is also proving to be self-consuming. This is amplified by the specific ground rules in our economy which preclude morals and ethics, leading to predation and bending of the rules by those who have gained success and power.

This warping of the playbook to maintain their advantage intentionally prevents healthy competition and leads to unfair exploitation of those who did not achieve the power positions in the earlier state of evolution of the Capitalistic society.

CONSEQUENCES OF A CONTROLLED GOVERNMENT

With the government controlled by the predators via the wielding of both power and money, the system ceases to function as it was intended because there is no longer a governing body to define rules that include the morals and ethics necessary to allow levels of creativity that lead to an advanced, successful society.

It appears we have now reached that stage in the United States with our Congress consumed by their own ambitions and largely controlled by the lobbying efforts of corporations.

WHAT WE NEED TO DO NOW

Does that mean we need a revolution? Hardly, it was the promise of reward that led to advancements in our society, so upending the whole system would not likely make the world a better place or provide more opportunity. We need to begin by *quiet-quitting* in these corporations that are not respecting their workers. We need to protest all aspects of government that support these corporations through allocation of our tax dollars.

We need the silent working majority to make a firm stand such that the creative, hard driving individuals that made this country a world leader in nearly every field and form of technology will no longer be stifled and once again see reward for their personal risks and efforts.

The only way to do this is to remove the corporations' government granted sense of entitlement to take more than they give with respect to the individuals that make them up. This will require upending the accepted norm of coveting and granting privilege to the wealthy who are now oppressing a sufficient majority of the creative population.

For this task, we look to the highly motivated millennials to ramp up their efforts and pass it on to the next generations before they also reach that age and level of success that reduced the baby boom generation from an idealistic young majority to an aging, greedy, wealthy, and self-serving conglomeration.

Imagine for a moment, a system where ethics and morals are one with the word "business", a system where the quality of human lives, employees, and product or service quality stand above profits on the metric scale. A system where workers are compensated fairly and the government does not impose increased taxes on the middle class to supplement the lower income class for basic needs while removing these responsibilities from the corporations who employ them.

The greed driven sociopathic leaders we find in corporations today will no longer have a place in the world. Imagine a system where MBAs are trained to serve the industry they are in for a sustainable long-term future with the happiness of company employees as the primary metric governing every corporate decision.

Unfortunately, it is only you the employees of these corporations who are in a position to carry the message of change to them.

Reimagine the future to create a non-exploitive, sustainable form of capitalism and together we will continue to build a limitless, creative society with infinite potential.

Reclaim your life as your own. The time to *quiet-quit* is now.

REVIEWS MAKE THE DIFFERENCE

I am eternally grateful to you for taking the time to read this and hope it has provided tools that will help you find meaning in your journey through life. If you found this content useful, one way to pay it forward is to let others know by leaving an online review. Your thoughts help others determine if this book might help them reach their goals, and it is very rewarding for me to know that this work has benefitted others. I personally read all the reviews because your feedback helps me empower others and improve how I can best communicate this important information.

Thanks again for your support!

ACKNOWLEDGEMENTS

Without the contributions of thoughtful friends, reviewers, and people with more wisdom than myself, I would not be able to organize and complete my thoughts. Thank you to Brian Benedetti, George Thompson, Cathy Kelley, and Floyd Majors who have been called upon more than they deserve to review my writings and have always, when needed, gently nudged me back on track to help me communicate my message. Special thanks to Gary Keeler for saving my opening paragraph and offering prudent thoughts on Buddhism. I'm blessed to have all of you in my life.

Thank you to my parents who taught me to think independently.

Finally, thank you to nature and humanity for great Literature, Art, and Diversity all of which give me faith that the positives of mankind will prevail over the primordial negative forces inherent in our evolving species, and all of which keep me motivated to continue writing.

CONTACT THE AUTHOR

daleefunk@gmail.com

https://www.amazon.com/author/dale_e_funk

MORE BOOKS BY DALE E FUNK

If you gained insight from this book, you might enjoy his other books found on Amazon Kindle.

"NO SHAME – The Key to Weight Loss" addresses the real reasons we have difficulty losing weight and how to avoid falling into the trap of paying for endless diets.

"NO SHAME – The Key to the Fountain of Youth" is a handbook for staying active, enjoying exercise, and preventing injury throughout life without the need for expensive equipment and personal trainers.

REFERENCES

1.)   Peters, T., Waterman, R. (1982, Jan 1). *In Search of Excellence: Lessons from America's Best Run Companies.* New York, Harper & Rowe

2.)   Chamorro-Premuzic, T. (2013, April 10). *Does Money Really Affect Motivation? A Review of the Research.* Harvard Business Review. https://hbr.org/2013/04/does-money-really-affect-motiv

3.)   Pink, D. (2010, April 1). *RSA: Animate: The Surprising Truth about What Motivates Us.* www.theRSA.org , https://www.youtube.com/watch?v=u6XAP nuFjJc

4.)   Sinek, S. () *.Most Leaders Don't Even Know the Game They're In.* https://www.youtube.com/watch?v=RyTQ5-SQYTo

5.) Kilgore, T. (2022, Jan 31). *Starbucks CEO Kevin Johnson's Total Compensation Rose 39% in 2021 to $20.4 Million*, MarketWatch, marketwatch.com, https://www.marketwatch.com/story/starbucks-ceo-kevin-johnsons-total-compensation-rose-39-in-2021-to-204-million-2022-01-31

6.) Sainato, M. (2020, Feb 5). 'I'm not a robot': Amazon Workers Condemn Unsafe, Grueling Conditions at Warehouse. Theguardian.com, https://www.theguardian.com/technology/2020/feb/05/amazon-workers-protest-unsafe-grueling-conditions-warehouse

7.) Santora, S. (2022, Nov 16). Elon Musk's Twitter Ultimatum, 'Exactly Why We Need More Unions': Internet. On The Internet, newsweek.com, Newsweek, Source: https://www.newsweek.com/elon-musk-twitter-ultimatum-exactly-why-need-more-unions-internet-1760173

8.) Dong-hyuk, H., (2009), Squid Game, (television drama series), Netflix 2019, https://en.wikipedia.org/wiki/Squid_Game

9.) Makarry M., Daniel, M., (2016, May 3) Study Suggests Medical Errors Now Third Leading Cause of Death in the U.S. hopkinsmedicine.org, John Hopkins Medicine. Retrieved online

10.) Wikipedia, Oprah Winfrey, (no date) https://en.wikipedia.org/wiki/Oprah_Winfrey

11.) Weiner, E. (2015, April 8). *Bhutan's Dark Secret to Happiness.* www.bbc.com., BBC Travel. https://www.bbc.com/travel/article/20150408-bhutans-dark-secret-to-happiness

12.) 2020 Population Review, Happiest Countries in the World 2023. worldpopulationreview.com. https://worldpopulationreview.com/country-rankings/happiest-countries-in-the-world

13.) *Bhutan's Gross National Happiness Index.* University of Oxford. Oxford Poverty and Human Development Initiative. Retrieved from: https://ophi.org.uk/policy/gross-national-happiness-index/

14.) Ura, K., Alkire, S., Zangmo, T., Wangdi, K., (May 2012). *An Extensive Analysis of GNH Index*. Centre for Bhutan Studies. https://ophi.org.uk/extensive-analysis-of-gnh-index/

15.) Malinsky, G., (Aug, 2022). *Don't try quiet quitting says Kevin O'Leary: it's a 'really bad idea'*. CNBC make it. https://www.cnbc.com/2022/08/20/kevin-oleary-quiet-quitting-is-a-really-bad-idea.html

16.) World Population review., (2023). *Suicide Rate by Country 2023*. https://worldpopulationreview.com/country-rankings/suicide-rate-by-country

17.) World Population Review., (2023) *Median Income by Country 2023*. https://worldpopulationreview.com/country-rankings/median-income-by-country

18.) Vanttinen, P. (2020, Dec 1). *Finland Hit by a New Wave of Drug Abuse.*, Euractive. https://www.euractiv.com/section/politics/short_news/finland-hit-by-a-new-wave-of-drug-use/

19.) Metz, S., Mormon Church Fined $5M for Obscuring Size of Portfolio, AP The Associated Press, retrieved online https://apnews.com/article/mormonism-us-securities-and-exchange-commission-religion-business-a598c9ef9544f57e0b60d5ca80774bf7

20.) Mark, J., (2021, July 22). *Four Noble Truths.* World History Encyclopedia. https://www.worldhistory.org/Four_Noble_Truths/

21.) Wang, C., (2022, Oct. 21). *The Four Noble Truths of Buddhism Explained & Its Significance to Your Spirituality.* Buddah & Karma. https://buddhaandkarma.com/blogs/guide/the-four-noble-truths-explained

22.) Sweet, K., (2022, Dec. 20). *Wells Fargo to Pay $3.7B Over Consumer Law Violations*, AP, Yahoo Finance, Retrieved from Yahoo Finance on 2/23/2023: https://finance.yahoo.com/news/wells-fargo-pay-3-7b-141425130.html

23.) Damania, Z., (2020), Stop Silencing Doctors: A Clinician Manifesto., YouTube., Vlog - ZDoggMD, https://www.youtube.com/watch?v=Mvlqh0JN55M